THE MĀNOA GANG

REMEMBRANCES OF OLD HAWAI'I
AND OBSERVATIONS ON LIFE IN GENERAL

GEORGE FRANCIS COLLINS

Order this book online at www.trafford.com
or email orders@trafford.com

Most Trafford titles are also available at major online book retailers.

Print information available on the last page.

ISBN: 978-1-4907-5266-2 (sc)
ISBN: 978-1-4907-5268-6 (hc)
ISBN: 978-1-4907-5267-9 (e)

Library of Congress Control Number: 2014922290

Trafford rev. 02/26/2015

 www.trafford.com
North America & international
toll-free: 1 888 232 4444 (USA & Canada)
fax: 812 355 4082

CONTENTS

ACKNOWLEDGEMENTS

A special thanks to Herbert Kawainui Kane for his help in accumulating these stories on his computer for me, to Carla Brown for typing, and to Lelehua Yuen for initially editing the book.

Aloha and mahalo to Normita Error for putting the manuscript on her computer and providing me with working copies.

Much love and thanks to my daughters KC Collins and Sarah Amico for reorganizing and editing The Mānoa Gang.

This book is dedicated to Eva Anita Rodiek.

A FEW WORDS BEFORE YOU GET STARTED

It seems that most of us after surviving a half-century, (in my case more than 80 years), like to tell stories about how things were in the good old days.

For more than three years I have written short stories about old and new Hawai'i for a local newsletter. As a result, I have been encouraged to record my memories of growing up in the Hawaiian Islands, particularly those about Mānoa Valley on the island of O'ahu, even more.

This book is written solely for your enjoyment. In many instances, names are mentioned in order to tell a true story, and are not meant to he harmful in any way to anyone, living or dead.

The Mānoa Gang*

Pake Ah Leong
Roger Monsarrat
Shaw Nash
Sonny Bordner
Cecil Saunders
Billy King
Chico Gibson
George Medeiros
George Magoon
Jackie Wailua Midkiff
Mae Carden
Betty Crozier
Billy Barnhart
Bobbie Hagood
Frank Wooley
Bobbie Grimshaw
Bunt Gorlangton

Chris Faria
Johnny Nash
Cliff Bailey
Snooky Bordner
Billy Saunders
Mifflin Thomas
Jack Porteus
Cliff Bailey
Martha Jean Midkiff
Ronald Frazier
Margie Crozier
Barbara Jean Jeffries
George Collins
Blakie Lightfoot
Scotchie Walker
Sonny Gorlangton
Helen Duryea

*Raymond Mant, Lex Brodie, the Bowmans, Eldbridge Durant, and others would have been included in the list above, but they were as much as five years older. And then there were a whole bunch of guys who were "too young."

It is likely I have omitted the names of some members of the Mānoa Gang. I apologize if this has happened and suggest you add your name to the list.

Home of the Mānoa Gang

The Nuʻuanu Trolley

My aunt Pauline Rodiek told me that in the late 1890's and early 1900's, ladies from the big homes along Nuʻuanu Avenue went shopping in downtown Honolulu on a horse-drawn trolley.

The trolley had open sides and the women all carried umbrellas in case of rain. The driver would stop at most houses along the way and clang his bell to let the ladies in the houses know he was waiting. Most of the trolley passengers knew each other well and could tell the driver if Mrs. so-and-so was going to town that day.

Electric trolleys came in at a later date, still with open sides, but with cowcatchers. I used to ride home on these streetcars from Punahou School in the afternoons. In those days it cost a nickel to ride, and since the streetcars were almost always crowded, I used to ride the cowcatcher in the rear, or as far away from the conductor as I could get.

The conductor would get mighty huhū (angry) with his free-loaders, so we would usually drop off near Lanihuli Drive at the top of Punahou hill. It wasn't too long of a walk home from there, and I could spend my nickel carfare on shaved ice, sweet ice cubes (three per bag), or some crack seed.

Kailua, Oʻahu in the '20's to '30's

In the 1920s it used to take a couple of hours for the family to drive over the Pali from Honolulu to Kailua beach. Usually there was charcoal-broiled steak, and chicken or squab, along with succulent Kailua-grown corn on the cob, rolls from the Young Hotel bakery, and all sorts of other good things to eat.

We spent a lot of time in the ocean bodysurfing, sometimes holding onto short two-foot pine-wood boards. When catching a wave, you took a deep breath, put your head down, and by the time you ran out of air, you would be high and dry on the beach.

Many of the Kailua residents had horses and often we would ride along the beach or mauka (toward the mountains) of Kalaheo Avenue. This would take us through thorny lantana, but by lying down and keeping our legs on the top of the horses' 'ōkole (rear end); we wouldn't scratch our bare legs and feet on the lantana bushes.

Since the horses didn't object, we assumed that the lantana thorns did not bother them.

Between the lantana and Kawainui swamp was what we called the "pine forest." I guess there were a couple hundred acres of ironwood trees growing there. Next to the ironwoods on the Kalama side toward Kāne'ohe, was a huge grove of coconut trees (a failed copra venture). Today its called the Coconut Grove area of Kailua. I still think about those times when I rode through the whispering pines, interrupted only by the occasional snorting of a horse.

Electricity was limited to electric lights in those days. Rice and other food was cooked on kerosene stoves. There were no Frigidaires. Blocks of ice were bought for iceboxes, either at Date's Tavern or Kalapawai Store. Telephones were the early primitive kind, and the people living along the beach road in Kailua had their special phone rings, like two short and three long.

People pretended not to listen in to calls made to friends and acquaintances in other houses, but I remember in every Kailua house I was ever in, there was always a mad dash to pick up the phone and listen in on the latest gossip. The telephone operator knew what was going on more than anyone else, of course.

There were three stores in Kailua in those days. Driving into Kailua the first one was Date's Tavern. The groceries and sundries part of it was right on the corner by the intersection, and the store was entered by climbing up about six wooden steps which curved around the front. The merchandise for sale was comparable to one of today's 7-Elevens, except everything was much cheaper.

Packages of Wing cigarettes were 10 cents and were preferred over the dry, homemade, needle-like ironwood leaves rolled up in newspaper, that at best produced only tears and coughs.

On the Ku'ulei Street-side of Date's Tavern was the entrance to the large banquet or party area. This was always very busy on Saturday nights. It was open to the breezes on one side overlooking a Japanese-style garden island surrounded by a large carp pond.

A number of years later, when I was about 15, we were drinking Asahi beer in the tavern and one of our group, David Withington, got into the carp pool and caught some live baby carp which he swallowed whole, with a beer chaser. He did this because he had read that a cousin of his at Yale had started a goldfish-swallowing contest.

Next door, on the Kāne'ohe side of Date's Tavern, was the huge bird cage where Date's doves were housed. I remember waiting while a dozen or so birds were caught, killed, defeathered, eviscerated, and then cut in half for our Sunday barbeques. A great show for us young kids.

Just beyond the Tavern towards Mōkapu, on Kailua Road, was Gouveia's Portuguese sausage place. The sausage was smoked for a couple of days out in the open, hanging over burning green kiawe wood. The smoke, full of garlic and meat odors, smelled wonderful.

About two miles down South Kaleheo from Kailua Road, on the beach road toward Lanikai, you came to an intersection. On the beach side was Kalapawai Market, a very small Chinese store that we called "Richard's" after the owner's son. The two important things they sold there, that I remember, were ice and sometimes good sirloin steaks.

The blocks of ice came rumbling out of a big square box after you fed quarters into a slot on its side. I marveled at the science of a machine which could shoot a 25 pound block of ice down a carpet-lined chute just by putting a quarter into the slot! I would have liked to have ridden down the chute except that I might have gotten stuck inside the box somewhere and frozen to death.

Another store, just a block away towards the Pali and Campos' Dairy, was Akai's store. It later became Lanikai store and, later still, a large Foodland grocery store. A jovial Hawaiian lady, Mrs. Elizabeth Akai, was the proprietor of this small store which sold mostly canned goods and candy. It was also the post office for the community.

The left front of the store looked like an egg crate, with one or two hundred small square holes opened from outside the store, each with its combination lock. Inside the store, the holes were open so you could ask a child or a friend to pick up your mail from Mrs. Akai.

At the back of the store was a curtain of long strings of beads that kept a person from within the store from seeing too much of what was going on behind it. We could see that there was a lie-down place and Mr. Akai was usually lying down there, either asleep or puffing on a long opium pipe. We were never nervy enough to ask about this small opium den.

Mrs. Akai was noted for her wonderful lau lau (fat pork and butterfish wrapped in taro leaves and then wrapped again in ti leaves for steaming). Later, after selling out her store to the Lau family, Mrs. Akai sold lau lau and poi in cans under her own label. You could even get these delicacies in stores on the coast of California, which was about as far as our thinking went in those days.

I am not sure if Akai was Elizabeth's real name or not. Akai means "by the sea" in Hawaiian, and the store was about 200 yards from the ocean.

In 1946 we moved into a Lanikai beach house and did most of our grocery shopping at Lanikai Store. It was located where Akai's store had been many years before. A tough old broad, Mrs. Lau, owned and ran the place. It's a wonder that Lanikai Store stayed alive.

Vegetables, like lettuce, were picked over and sold down to the last leaf. The beet and carrot tops were always wilted and hanging lifelessly in their bins. Long skinny carrots were so rubbery they could almost bend in half without breaking. Whenever Mrs. Lau was behind the meat counter, the hanging scale was held steady by the downward weight of Mrs. Lau's thumb. She removed her thumb from the scale at the same instant that she lifted off the meat so you could never be sure how much meat or thumb weight you were buying.

There was, however, a bright light at the end of the tunnel, as far as the Lanikai Store was concerned. Maurice "Sully" Sullivan, who had managed the non-commissioned officer's club at Pearl Harbor during World War II, ran the liquor department. Besides being in love with Mrs. Lau's daughter, whom he later married, he gave us good prices on the considerable amount of booze we purchased in those days.

Sully went on to open up 18 or more Foodlands for Mrs. Lau and her Chinese hui. I was told he received a $1,000 monthly bonus for every new store he opened.

KAILUA GAMES & MUCH, MUCH MORE

About once or twice a month we would go over to the Henshaw's house in Kailua. I was about five years old and remember what a long haul it was over the Pali, and so windy at the top you felt like you were going to blow over any minute. The top did blow off many a convertible.

Mother usually took along an upside-down cake, or spaghetti into which she had already mixed the sauce. Other guests and family brought things like watermelon and corn. Uncle Kelly Henshaw grilled chicken, steak or squab. The latter were raised in a huge cage by Tom Date (pronounced "dottie") behind his store.

In those early days in Kailua, cooking was done on a kerosene stove, and we had to bring over big glass jugs of drinking water and blocks of ice for the icebox. The Sherwood Lowry house next door to the Henshaws' generated their electricity with a windmill. "Uncle Sherwood"– everybody was "Uncle" or "Auntie" this or that – had a spit, and would employ his children, and those of us next door, to turn a whole lamb round and round using Portuguese energy -- "manual" power.

We were at the beach, in and out of the water, all day long. Boys and girls both wore heavy, one-piece, swim suits and we had short, pine wood surfboards to ride the fast waves at Kailua.

Aside from the fringe of beach houses, Kailua was mainly a huge grove of coconut and pine trees (ironwoods). We almost choked to death trying to smoke pine needles.

There were so few people living along the beach back then that often you could look up and down the beach and see no one for miles. One day my pal Johnny Nash and I were moseying out to the beach and we stopped short in shocked amazement.

Girls!

But these weren't just any girls. These were older girls we knew from school who were about three grades (eighth or ninth grade) ahead of us. They had abandoned their swimming garb and were dashing to and fro and jumping up and down in the waves.

Johnny and I ducked down behind an outrigger canoe and peeked around its bow at the girls. Funniest thing we'd ever seen. We looked around and spotted where they had tossed their bathing suits. So one, two, three, we dashed down the beach, grabbed the suits and made off with them, dropping them behind the canoe.

The girls knew who the culprits were, of course, and were mad as hell. But one brave girl, I think it was Dotsie S., just marched right out of the surf and retrieved all of the bathing suits.

LET'S GO BACK IN TIME....

THE HAWAIIAN FLAG

Visitors to our shores frequently ask why our Hawaiian State flag combines the British Union Jack with stripes like those seen in the flag of the United States. The answer is of some historical significance.

Although flags were not traditional among the Polynesians, after King Kamehameha conquered all of the islands, he felt he needed one (a flag) to discourage foreign nations who had begun to cast covetous eyes at his kingdom. Friendly British advisors suggested that the Union Jack be flown over the royal palace in Honolulu both as a sign of British friendship and as a warning to predator nations to keep away. The war of 1812 complicated things, though, and with many Americans then in Hawai'i, it was suggested Kamehameha establish a flag of his own.

Captain George Beckley, an English sea captain, was chosen to design a new flag, and his happy solution to the problem was to combine the British Union Jack with stripes like those seen in the American flag. The eight stripes were symbolic of the eight major Hawaiian Islands.

So our present flag has flown over us as a kingdom, a republic, a territory of the United States, and with the coming of statehood, as the state flag of Hawai'i.

SWEET TOOT - SUGAR, THE LIFE BLOOD OF HAWAI'I

1778 - Captain James Cook found a honey-bearing reed at Ewa, O'ahu.

1779 - The great haole, Captain Cook make (killed) at Kealakekua, Hawai'i.

1794 - Kamehameha formally ceded the islands of Hawai'i to Great Britain.

1795 - Kamehameha I pursued his favorite sport - war - and conquered all the islands except Kaua'i. That island was saved temporarily when Kamehameha's war fleet was destroyed by a storm.

1802 - The first sugar was processed by Chinese on the island of Lana'i.

KAMEHAMEHA'S GENERALS

In 1790 Isaac Davis arrived in Hawai'i as a mate on a small American schooner. The ship was captured and all of the crew drowned, except Davis, who after much torture was allowed to stay in the islands. He had been carried ashore blind and it was 18 months before he recovered his sight.

John Young arrived in the islands at the same time as Davis. He was attached to Kamehameha (along with Davis). For their knowledge of firearms, they were given the status of chiefs. They were more trusted by the king than the native chiefs. So, when Davis accompanied Kamehameha to O'ahu, Young was left behind as Governor of Hawai'i, where he lived very much like the natives.

(Interesting excerpt from P. Campbell's book, Voyage Around the World.)

ECOLOGY IN THE 1800's

In the early 1800's, whaling ships began to reduce the whale population in Hawaiian waters. On Hawai'i island, at that time, there were about 3,000 residents in the small town of Kawaihae. Streetlights were fueled with whale oil and there was even a jail in this small town.

Over in Honolulu, Don Francisco Marin, a Portuguese botanist, planted pineapple, guava, mango, coffee, tobacco, grains, cotton and grapes. Grape arbors were an enjoyable resting place for early Portuguese residents in Hawai'i. The grapes, which were the Isabella variety, are still grown today, and that's how Vineyard Street in Honolulu got its name.

BULL DURHAM

There was no real "R&R" for labor in Hawai'i in the 1800's, and a 60-hour work week was considered normal.

In an attempt to make life just a little easier for people, Bull Durham, a roll-your-own cigarette tobacco, was introduced to Hawai'i's hard-working plantation laborers by H. Hackfeld & Co., Ltd. Hackfeld was one of the "Big Five" plantation agents at the time, and was the predecessor of today's Amfac.

Thus, Bull Durham provided local workers with inexpensive relaxation, while at the same time providing the Hackfeld Company with some tidy profits.

This very affordable tobacco came in a small cotton bag with drawstrings at the top. A small packet containing about 20 unbleached, orangish-colored, roll-your-own cigarette papers were lightly glued to the bag, and there was a dark-blue label with a bull pictured on it wrapped around both the bag and the packet of papers.

It took two fingers on each hand to open the tobacco pouch. The smoker then sprinkled out a sufficient amount of the finely-chopped tobacco with one hand onto one of the orange-colored cigarette papers, which he held with the other hand, between his thumb and third finger, while depressing the center of the paper with the index finger of the same hand. At the same time, tobacco was poured from the pouch and carefully jiggled to spread the tobacco evenly in the trough.

While holding the paper with the tobacco on it with one hand, the smoker then closed the pouch by pulling the bag strings with the two fingers of his other hand and with his teeth. Got a clear picture of that?

Then, since wind or other untoward problems could arise, the smoker quickly put the closed bag of Bull Durham into a shirt pocket with one hand, and while holding the exposed tobacco on the paper, he carefully but swiftly licked the long edge on one side of the cigarette paper and, with both hands, tightly rolled the tobacco inside the paper, sealing the wet edge onto the dry edge of the paper. This "spit" glue hopefully held until the cigarette had been consumed. One end was quickly twisted while the other open end of the cigarette was held between the lips.

Then, lighting a match by striking it on the seat of one's pants, our smoker lit up his smoke (cigarette). This was a lot easier than scratching a wooden Lancer safety match on the side of the matchbox.

In either case, the burnt match was saved rather than simply tossed away, in order to keep from starting a fire. Burnt matches were slid back into a matchbox with the hot end placed at the opposite end of the unlit heads of matches a smoker kept in his pocket.

Now, picture yourself riding along on your favorite Appaloosa at a fast cowboy trot, lighting up your own roll-your-own Bull Durham cigarette while holding on to the reins between the fourth and pinkie finger of one hand for horse control.

If your cigarette had gone out, it was one thing; but if you had been trotting along on your favorite steed and your lips started to burn, at all costs you could not drop the hot butt alongside the trail. You either squashed the burning end between your thumb and index finger or you tried to put it out on the saddle. There was some risk here for the cowboy setting his crotch on fire.

Occasionally, a smoker would put a hot match the wrong way into the matchbox, and a sudden huge flare up would occur when the "business" end of the live matches all caught on fire at once. This frequently caused painful burns, along with singed chest hairs.

If you had been smoking a Bull Durham cigarette while reading this, by now your lips would be on fire.

The major reason for my calling Bull Durham to your attention is to point out that, in the evolution of profanity from the time I was a little squirt some 80-plus years ago, you could say 'Bull Durham' safely in front of your mother, but not the other two-word bull expression.

Nowadays, at least here in America, you can say almost anything in front of your mother without fear of receiving nine lashes or being made to eat soap. And that's no Bull Durham.

THE GREAT MAHELE OF 1848

Hawai'i was an absolute monarchy under Kamehameha I, as well as under his son and successor, Liholiho. Only the king owned the land, and he owned it all. Some of his chiefs held life tenancy to property which reverted back to the crown upon their death.

Under Kamehameha III, the kingdom became a constitutional monarchy. This change led to the Great Mahele of 1848, which partitioned the lands of the kingdom fairly equally between the crown, the government and the chiefs. The chiefs were to provide land in fee for lesser chiefs, who in turn were to provide land to commoners living on their land. The sale of crown or government lands was forbidden by amendment to the Great Mahele Act.

When Kamehameha III died, the only lineal descendant of Kamehameha I was Princess Bernice Pauahi Bishop. She was married to Charles R. Bishop, a banker and a businessman, and was herself a prominent social and civic leader. Gradually, she inherited large tracts of land from the chiefs of the Kamehameha dynasty. These then were the Crown Lands of Hawai'i.

Princess Pauahi never forgot her royal lineage, and so through her will, she used her inherited properties for the advancement of the

Hawaiian people by forming the Bernice Pauahi Bishop Estate. The income from this estate supports the Kamehameha Schools.

EARLY MISSIONARY INFLUENCE ON EDUCATION

Hawaiians, like many early cultures, didn't have a written language, making it quite difficult to gain access into their true history. Facts, beliefs and stories were passed from one generation to another by word of mouth and became altered according to the will of the teller.

Until early American missionaries decided it would be a good idea to translate spoken Hawaiian into a written language, Hawai'i's history was remembered by the people of that generation, or what could be found in the log books and journals of early explorers of the Pacific such as Captain Cook.

Historians were missionaries themselves, or writers who were influenced by missionaries, such as John Papa I'i, the great recorder of Hawaiian history, who received both his education and religious training from missionaries.

Polynesian dress (or undress) and hula dancing were thought to be lewd and lascivious by the elders of the Congregational Church. Their influence was so great that Hawaiian songs written at the time followed the musical tempo of such lively hymns as Nearer My God To Thee.

This overly protective influence by the missionaries over the Hawaiian population continued almost halfway through the 1900s. An example of this protective interest was that a swimming pool was deemed unhealthy, therefore none was provided when the new Kamehameha Schools were built on O'ahu in the 30s. Also, classes in hula dancing were not provided. It was some time after World War II before college preparatory classes were available to more than five percent of the "brighter" Kamehameha School students. The big thing for boys attending the school was instruction in manual skills. Male students at Kamehameha spent two senior years with half of that time devoted to working for businesses in the community.

Graduating males were hired by local utility companies, and graduating females, who were trained extensively in homemaking skills, were expected to go home. Fortunately, this early-misguided influence on the Hawaiian people has disappeared.

Pīkake (Hawaiian Peacocks and Flowers)

Pīkake is the phonetic spelling of the Hawaiian word for "peacock." Peacocks were imported and treasured as pets in the early days of the Kingdom. Besides blues, rare white peacocks were brought into Hawai'i.

Someone gave the Hinds at Pu'uwa'awa'a Ranch some white peacocks. These were marvelous birds, but their loud screeching was enough to wake the dead, let alone keep trespassers away.

The peacock noise was just too overwhelming, so, the story goes, Mona Hind ordered her cowboys to take the birds out and shoot them. But the cowboys did not have the heart to kill the birds, and they were let go way up mauka (in the mountains).

Today on the Big Island, many wild peacocks, both blues and whites, can be seen mauka of the belt highway from the Hue Hue Ranch to Pu'uwa'awa'a Ranch on the Kona-side of the Big Island.

Princess Ka'iulani, the beloved daughter of King Kalakaua's sister, was next in line to inherit Hawai'i's throne after Kalakaua. But tragically, this beautiful princess died young.

While she was alive, Princess Ka'iulani became very much attached to some rare pure white peacocks (pīkake) and so became fondly known as the "Princess of the Peacocks." Her favorite flower was the sweet-smelling Chinese Jasmine, and since it had no Hawaiian name, her friends named it pīkake in her honor.

The pearl-shaped white pīkake flower is still an island favorite. So give your sweetie a pīkake lei today.

Some Helpful Local Words

Lōlō - feeble minded - generally used to describe dear friends.

Pupule - insane - same as above - a lolo buggah!

Huli - to turn or change. In tennis you huli when you change sides of the net. In cooking you huli the steak from one side to the other.

Lalo - down, or downward. Put down that rock! Lalo your 'ōkole (fanny) close to mine.

Luna - high, over, the boss, ie. George W. Bush, me.

Ho'okupu - tribute, tax, ceremonial gift. Used when I grew up mostly as the name given to a pot-luck dinner

Malo - Traditionally, the Hawaiian man's loincloth. As in the song: "He wore a malo and a coconut hat; one was for this and the other for that."

   Pololei - straight, correct, right. In politics, you usually say, "That guy's no pololei."

   Mane'o - itchy, prickly, sexually titillating. A song: When You're Feeling Mane'o.

LANGUAGE BARRIERS

Pearly Toots
Question: "Auwē, teeta, mahea your pearly toots?"
Answer: "My toots hale stay, next time I bring."
   Translation:
Question: "My goodness, good-looking, where are your pearly teeth?"
Answer: "My teeth are at home. I will bring them the next time we meet."

The Wherewithal
Question: "Eh blahla (Pre-WWII word for 'brother,' with a Filipino twist--sometimes shortened to 'blah'), were you was been stay?"
Answer: "To tal da troot, Auntie Pinau's place I was at."
   Translation:
Question: "Hey, brother, where have you been?"
Answer: "To tell you the truth, I was at Auntie Pinau's house."

Let There Be Light
"An wen you pau da room, make shua you close da light."
   Translation:
"When you leave the room, be sure to turn off the light."

"Maka piapia da eye, but before time was good-lookin."
   Translation:
"My eyesight is poor now. but I could see well in the past."

Other Translations
"Pehea 'Oe?" = "How are you?" (Hawaiian to English)
"Pehui?" = "How are you?" (Filipino to English)
"Maika'i no" = "Very good." (Hawaiian/Filipino to English)

Social Security

Question: "How many years you make?"
Answer: "Last year this time, 65 years I make."

Question: "You can write?"
Answer: "No can write."

LISTEN TO THE TRAIN

In the good-old days, the O'ahu Railroad and Land Company passenger trains went almost all the way around O'ahu. Besides going to the hotel resort in Hale'iwa, you could go on beyond to Waialua, Kahuku, or even further to get away from it all.

In addition to hauling bagged sugar to Honolulu for shipment to Crockett, California, the railroad was the best source of transportation to and from the big city for people living and working on the plantations..

It so happened that Manuel Souza and Maria Gomes of Kahuku Plantation decided to go to the Royal (the old Royal Hawaiian Hotel in downtown Honolulu), for their honeymoon. After their wedding and a huge lū'au, they quietly slipped away, just the two of them, in time to catch the OR&L passenger train to Honolulu.

The train was a little behind schedule that day, and Manuel, who had loaded up on everything at the lū'au, including his Auntie Pinau's Portuguese bean soup, was having some gastric pain. Upon loudly, but unavoidably expelling some air, he immediately attempted to cover up his accident by exclaiming to his bride. "Eh, Marie, you hear the whistle?" To which Marie replied, "No, Manuel, but I smell the smoke."

A TOUCH OF HISTORY

In 1803, Spanish cowboys and horses landed at Kawaihae on Hawai'i to care for the gift of cattle given to Kamehameha by Captain George Vancouver in 1794.

By 1804, construction of Kamehameha's fleet of double-hulled war canoes, built on Hawai'i, was complete. The king was ready to attack Kaua'i for the second time from O'ahu. The plan was abandoned, however, when a terrible pestilence, thought to be cholera or bubonic plague, wiped out about half of the people on O'ahu.

In 1810, to avoid inevitable conquest, Kaumuali'i, the ruling chief on Kaua'i, ceded Kaua'i and Ni'ihau to Kamehameha.

In 1811, the sandalwood trade boomed between Hawai'i and Macao and Canton.

THE WAR (WORLD WAR I THAT IS) - HITS HOME

By 'hits home' I don't mean that a bomb dropped on our roof in 1918, but it did hit home as far as my Uncle George F. Rodiek, his wife Aunt Pauline, and their family were concerned. Uncle George was the general manager of H. Hackfeld Co., Ltd., which was the largest of the "Big Five" companies in Hawai'i at the time. The position of German consul went with his job.

Just before 1917, anti-German sentiment had grown fairly high, peaking in Hawai'i where the Americans, British, and Japanese (then allies) greatly outnumbered those of German ancestry in the community. Rather than fighting the British at sea, a German gunboat, the Geier, docked at Honolulu, a neutral port at that time. The captain decided not to go out to sea to do battle with a Japanese battleship that was lying offshore waiting to pounce on it.

During its time in port, my uncle needed to go aboard the Geier, as he did on most German vessels which called at Hawaiian ports. In fact, Hackfeld & Co. Ltd. was a German firm and handled the ship's business, including turning it over upon seizure to the United States marshall. All of this helped the anti-German sentiment grow.

My Uncle George Rodiek was accused of being involved in a plot to foment a revolution against the British in India. Supposedly weapons for the rebels in India were being smuggled aboard a German ship - the Maverick, which had docked in Hilo. Although never proven, since Rodiek was German Consul, it was reasoned he was involved in the plot.

He was fined $10,000, and his American citizenship was revoked. He also spent a few days in jail. Years later he was pardoned by President Wilson who also restored his citizenship. But in 1917, under the Alien Custodian Act, Hackfeld & Co., Ltd. was taken over and its assets sold off to a group of Honolulu men for 10 cents on the dollar. It was renamed American Factors, Ltd., and a department store belonging to Hackfeld (B. F. Ehlers), was taken over and renamed Liberty House.

I remember Uncle George's lawyers, Bartley Crum and Martin Minney, visiting the Rodiek home after they moved to San

Francisco. There was always a good supply of 'ōkolehao (Hawaiian liquor) and gin which was homemade in a bathtub on the third floor of the house.

The San Francisco home, at the corner of Filmore and Broadway, was a gathering place for friends and relatives for years. Many evenings there would be 12 or more at the dinner table, not including Lita, the parrot. Sometimes the German language would crop up, as most jokes were told in German so those with small ears couldn't understand them.

Well, so much for that.

TRAVELING BY SHIP - SAN FRANCISCO TO HAWAI'I

Hawai'i roots were always tied closely to San Francisco, going as far back as the 1849 gold rush days. People traveled back and forth between Honolulu and San Francisco on sailing ships, which as time went on, gradually became combination steam-sailing vessels, and finally, the red-hulled Matson combination passenger-freight ships like the S.S. Maui, S.S. Wilhelmina, and the old S.S. Mānoa and S.S. Matsonia.

While I was conceived in Honolulu, I traveled to San Francisco with my mother of course, on the S.S. Maui, and came back a born Christian three weeks later with my mother and father on the S.S. Wilhelmina. I do not recall much about those initial voyages.

We went to California so I could be born there by caesarean section through the capable hands of Dr. Reginald Knight Smith. (When you have a name like 'Smith,' it is a good idea to stretch it out.) He had been my mother's family doctor when she was little. He practiced at the Mount Zion Hospital in San Francisco. My best friends have always said that my parents took home the wrong baby.

Later on, my mother and I traveled back to the mainland about every year and a half to visit relatives. It was always cold, and often foggy when we arrived in San Francisco. Tides in the bay were so strong it usually took two tugboats to help maneuver the ship alongside the dock. During this maneuver, a four-piece orchestra on deck would be playing a mournful rendition of California Here I Come.

After agricultural inspection, we would go on deck and look down at the grey, uninviting, passenger dock with its fairly small crowd of bundled-up, white-faced relatives and friends, anxiously looking up for a glimpse of the person, or persons, they were there to meet. No band, no lei, no warm, happy weather like Honolulu.

Arriving in Honolulu was an entirely different matter. The weather was warmer, of course, the seas and skies were bluer, and we were always up before dawn to try to get a glimpse of Maui and Molokai as we headed for Diamond Head and Honolulu Harbor. Just past Diamond Head, looking at Waikīkī or up Mānoa and Nuʻuanu valleys, was always a beautiful and happy sight.

Just outside of Kewalo Basin, the ship slowed and a couple of Young Bros. tugs, loaded with people bearing lei, began to pull alongside. It cost just $3.00 to ride out on a tug to greet the ship before it entered Honolulu Harbor. Anyone who was anyone came out. There were tour operators and small groups of Hawaiian musicians. Well, I could go on and on, but won't. It was just terribly exciting to see old friends this way.

Once inside the Harbor, the Royal Hawaiian Band would begin playing lovely music, while passengers would scurry to their staterooms below to do last-minute packing or labeling of suitcases and steamer trunks. By the time you went up on deck again, the ship was being tied up, and three gangways were being made fast to the ship. Before you knew it, you were on shore being smothered with kisses and lei.

George Francis Collins - Early Days

Our first house was on Lanihuli Drive at the top of Punahou Street in Mānoa. I remember a large bank of Mexican creepers (flowers) on the street side of the house. On the other side of the house was a lane with the Mānoa tennis courts just beyond. The Mexican creepers were full of bees, so of course I learned at an early age that bees sting!

My first recollection of a happening, even before I went to Miss Maxwell's preschool on Kewalo Street, was my being thrown out of a car, through the windshield, as the result of an accident on the corner of Punahou and Wilder Streets.

I was in my mother's lap, my father driving, when Dick Frazier's sister, who was intoxicated, drove across the street and banged into us. No safety glass or seat belts in those days. Dr. Alsup picked glass out of my head and wrapped the whole top of it up in gauze. The accident occurred at night and I could hardly wait for the next day to go out and show off my bandaged head to the neighborhood.

Our neighbors next door were Auntie Alice and Uncle Emil Waterman. Uncle Emil ran a tobacco store downtown. After 1932, and the repeal of prohibition, Mr. Waterman opened a liquor store. My dad used to get his straw-wrapped Perrier water, Poland-brand gin, and Pilsner Urquell beer from him.

Being an only child, I had to develop fun and games on my own sometimes. I remember one day I was fooling around with a sprinkler on the front lawn while my mother played bridge on the lānai with some lady friends. One of the women asked, "Georgie wouldn't throw that thing in here, would he'?" My mother replied, "Oh, no; he would never do a thing like that." Of course I did just that. Wet the ladies good! Hard shot, too, because you had to get whatever you were throwing over the lower lanai railing and between some huge baskets of maidenhair fern which were dangling from above.

Speaking of maidenhair fern, my mother was noted for her beautiful ferns, for which I was largely responsible. She used to mix my wee wee with water and sprinkle the ferns with it. Something to do with urine from a virgin. An old wives' tale, I'm sure.

While living on Lanihuli Drive, we had a Japanese maid by the name of Misae. She tried to discipline me for something by rubbing Hawaiian red pepper in my eyes. I didn't like Misae very much.

When I was about to enter the first grade, the family moved farther up in Mānoa Valley to a new home on Kahawai Street. It was a beautiful place on a hill overlooking taro patches and rice fields that grew all the way up the valley. No houses or streets to mar the view.

By 1930 the rice was almost all gone, and taro was all but eliminated a short time later. When I was a little older, the dried-up ditches provided great trenches for our World War I 'over the top' war games. We actually used Daisy BB guns (Benjamin pumps were not allowed), but quit when one boy was hit in the eye with a BB. Fortunately not too seriously.

Then we discovered another game for BB guns. There were a lot of kids who lived near us on lower Mānoa Road and so we declared war on them. We used to get them on the run, we with our guns and they with rocks. Of course, we felt we were the winners because of our superior firepower.

Some of the older boys in the neighborhood also played war with BB guns. Johnny Nash and I were spies for both sides. We were double agents, don't you know. Finally we got caught and were "shot!"

CHRISTMAS AT THE VOLCANO HOUSE

We spent several Christmas's at the old Volcano House in the early '30s – the large old place that was there before it burned to the ground. We usually stayed in a separate cottage to one side of the hotel but took our meals in the hotel dining room.

Getting to the Big Island from Oʻahu was not as easy as today. No airplanes. We traveled on inter-island vessels such as the S.S. Hualālai or the S.S. Waiʻaleʻale. If you had a tendency to get seasick, like my parents, you went right to bed as soon as you boarded. Although we went first class, the Inter-Island Steam Navigation Co. sold steerage tickets. This meant that early in the evening, mats provided by the company were lined up in the companionways outside the first class cabins.

Crossing the Molokaʻi channel, and passing windward of Maui, and down the Hāmākua Coast was usually quite rough. The Inter-Island's leviathans of the deep were top-heavy, so they pitched, rolled, and wallowed quite a lot. Outside the staterooms the steerage passengers were as miserable as we were, and listening to them throw up was contagious. It was not true that plain soda water, soda crackers, or green olives kept a person from getting seasick.

The trip started in Honolulu at four in the afternoon and you staggered off the ship in Hilo at 8am the next morning. Once I felt fine all the way over, but when I disembarked, the dock was moving up and down. It was then that I got seasick.

Finally, when you arrived in the cool volcano air about 35 miles from Hilo, all was well. It was great fun running up and down the long, closed-in veranda at the old Volcano House. There were always a lot of kids to play with. Trips to the sulphur bank and the steam bluffs were frequent. Usually there was at least one trip each to Thurston Lava Tube and the footprints. Out near the footprints, considerable heat could be felt near the surface of the lava, where we used to toast hot dogs and marshmallows at the ends of long sticks.

When the volcano was erupting at Halemaʻumaʻu, we would visit the pit at night looking for shapes in the red lines made by the lava as it cracked the cooler black lava surface. We always saw Madam Pele's image, and of course, outlines of chickens and other creatures.

Life in our little volcano cottage was interesting at times. I was the bar boy and often was sent over to the bar to pick up a bottle of "Old Rarity" scotch. It was 12-year-old scotch and cost $12 per bottle, and I was 12 years old. This was a source of great amusement for my father - "A dollar for each year." One evening when I returned with Old Rarity, my father and Aunt Nancy Wallace from Kona, were having a good fun war with bottles of carbonated seltzer water. Being as young as I was, I had not expected grownups to act so childishly.

The meals at the Volcano House were marvelous. Niolopa poha (gooseberry) jam and great big stacks of buttered toast went well with a big stack of hot cakes and syrup.

Once in a while we would ride horses at Haole Sumner's ranch house next to the Volcano golf course. The golf course had wire staked around the edge of the greens to keep the cattle off. Occasionally you would lose your golf balls down cracks in the lava on the fairways.

One Christmas morning about 6am, a hell of a noise was heard out on the porch right outside my window. There was such a clatter I threw up the blinds, but instead of eight tiny reindeer, there were about six Filipinos. They had come by to serenade the rich haole at the Volcano House. One musician, if I may use the word loosely, was playing the zither, and two others had guitars. How come "Silent Night" when it's daytime already? My father gave them some money to stop singing at our cottage. Ho, Ho, Ho.

Our trips to the volcano usually included a trip to Kona to visit friends of my parents. A couple of times we stayed at Nancy Wallace's in Kainaliu. She had no screens on the windows of her house so we all slept under mosquito nets for protection against the nasty critters. Nancy also had an old Japanese man who rode a Kona Nightingale (donkey) as he picked coffee berries from her trees. In front of him on the donkey were two cornucopia-shaped baskets which held the berries.

In the dry North Kona lava fields there are still wild Kona Nightingales. Today, a sign on the Queen Ka'ahumanu Highway near the Mauna Lani Resort has a picture of a jackass and a warning to watch for them crossing the road.

We stayed at the Kona Inn sometimes, traveling the Belt Road or Mamalahoa Highway, down to the beach via narrow Walua Road. Cars would sort of bend around each other as they passed. The Inter-Island Steam Navigation Co. in those days owned Kona Inn where they specialized in fresh swordfish (marlin) and beautiful sunsets.

Just past Hulihe'e Palace on the town side where the pier is today, Greenwell cowboys on horseback would run steers over the little beach, and into the water, for shipment to Honolulu. Quite colorful. Later there were cattle pens at the ocean end of Kailua pier where the pipi (beef) was loaded onto Young Brothers barges.

Unless you were visiting someone in Kamuela, or at a plantation on the Hāmākua Coast, it was faster to drive back to Hilo and your ship via the volcano from Kona.

I don't remember getting seasick on the way back to Honolulu on the ship. Funny, eh?

DANCING SCHOOLS IN HONOLULU

In the late '20's and early '30's, Honolulu was not very crowded. There were only two Collins names in the Mutual Telephone Company's book. We were there and so was the T.D. Collins family, to whom we were not related. Their house was three doors down from us on Lanihuli Drive in Mānoa Valley. This was just past the top of Punahou's Rocky Hill.

Some of the other Lanihuli Drive residents living on the same block were the O'Briens: Patsy and Junior, Nancy Knickerbocker, the Clark girls: Troy (a girl), Sweet, Ruth; and Marion Collins; and Major (Richard) and Mary Botts. On the corner next door to me lived the Watermans. Mr. Waterman played cribbage with some of the Castle & Cooke executives during lunch at the Pacific Club on weekdays.

But the piece de resistance was Madame Lester's house at the end of the block. It was here that we took our sweaty little hands to dancing school once a week for ballroom dancing lessons. It was a kind of a hateful thing to do for many of the boys, including me. And although we tried, we did not get away with hiding behind sofas and chairs. However, on a couple of occasions, I was lucky enough to escape by sneaking outside and hiding behind some huge 'ape (elephant ear) plants which grew under the eaves of her house.

Madame Lester had the blackest hair on both her head and her eyebrows. Since she grabbed the poorest dancers to demonstrate dance steps, such as the waltz and fox trot, I spent most of my time, when in her clutches, studying how much of her hair coloring was running down her face. She perspired a lot trying to push us clods around, so I forgave the workman-like odor which exuded from her large frame.

The next dancing school I attended was as prim and proper as those things could be in those days. It was run by Kay Singlehurst, Tommy's sister, and held in a theater-like building on Judd Street. I think it was called Kulamanu Studios. The ages of the students in the class ranged from 12 to 14, and all the boys had to dress alike in: white flannel pants, midnight blue sports jackets, white shirt, tie, shiny patent leather dancing shoes and white cotton gloves. Even though the boys wore gloves, we still had to hold a white handkerchief against our partner's back, which seemed a little ridiculous to me.

The girls wore a variation of evening and tea costumes, with patent leather shoes, white bobby socks, and white gloves. I remember a few of the plump girls wore 'stays' which I think meant, 'corset.' It's a good thing the plump boys didn't have to wear corsets or I would have been one of the first to go!

In spite of all the gussying up, the thing I remember most was that a few of the girls, and some of us boys, had terrible body odor.

There was a sort of post-graduate dancing school at the Royal Hawaiian Hotel where Ginny and Dan Wallace taught us the latest steps in ballroom dancing such as the tango. I wasn't there very long.

The "Pink Palace," the Royal Hawaiian, was where we went dancing to the music of Harry Owens' orchestra and other fine bands. The Wallaces put on a very graceful exhibition of sweeping ballroom dancing midway through the evening. The roof over the dance floor at the Royal rolled back and couples literally danced under the stars. The lights were low and we usually moved so slowly with our partners that dance steps were limited to rocking back and forth from one side to the other. Dancing, ha!

Dancing under the stars at the Royal Hawaiian was almost a weekly affair with the young crowd. Formal gowns and holokū (Hawaiian formal dress with train) on the girls, everyone of them with a beautiful flower lei, and the boys in white dinner jackets, pleated tuxedo shirts, ties, handkerchiefs, cummerbunds, cufflinks and studs with colors matching. I remember Tommy Arnott and George Maddams had the widest variety of colors.

The best part of the evening was when you could bury your face in the lei of your date and sniff up the perfume of the flowers as you danced a very slow Good Night Sweetheart.

THE LARGER WORLD

Mother used to push me to meet important visitors to

Hawai'i, although I used to rebel as much as I could. Some of these visitors are as follows:

Knute Rockne - football coach, "Are you going to play football for Notre Dame when you grow up?"

Ty Cobb - baseball great, "Are you going to play baseball when you grow up?"

Hoot Gibson - cowboy movie star, "Do you like horses?"

Jack Oakie - movie comedian, "Hey kid, get me another drink!"

Pendleton Roundup Indian Princess - pretty, but blank.

Don Blanding - poet and promoter of Lei Day is May Day in Hawai'i, wore white linen suits and drank Tom Collins cocktails.

Jay Gould - tycoon, "You can sit on my lap if you can find it."

'ULUPALAKUA RANCH

A little over a half century ago, 'Ulupalakua Ranch on Maui supplied the Honolulu market with prime beef, butter, eggs, ham and bacon. The big brown ranch eggs always tasted a lot better than the white ones, and the ranch bacon and butter were never rancid, as was much of the bacon and butter which came into Hawai'i by ship from the U.S. Mainland in those days.

My mother enjoyed visiting friends on the ranch, and one time when she traveled with me to Maui on either the S.S. Mauna Ke'a or the S.S. Haleakalā, the ship anchored off the beach (where the Prince Hotel is located today). Lifeboats were lowered and passengers and freight were rowed ashore through the surf. 'Ulupalakua cowboys carried the passengers and cargo from the shallow water to dry land, and the people rode horses for the long ride up to the ranch.

CASTLE SURF

South of Queen's Surf was Castle Surf where, during rough weather, a surfer could catch big waves and long rides on a surfboard. It was named after the Castles' beach home located on the town-side of the aquarium in Waikīkī, and directly onshore from the waves.

In the '20's we used to go swimming in the salt-water tank at the Castle home. There was a big hole with iron bars over it in the seawall to let the sea water surge inside the tank. Swimming pools were called "tanks" in those days. The water in the tank would rise and fall with the surge of the waves as it pushed the seawater in and sucked it out. Great fun, particularly on a rough day.

Later, when I surfed Castle, I looked in toward the shore nostalgically; remembering the good times I had in the Castle's tank when I was little.

DIVING IN KEALAKEKUA BAY

I visited the Frank Greenwell ranch in the late 20's and was thrilled to take part in shipping the Greenwell cattle from pens that were right next to the Captain Cook monument at Kealakekua. As you may know, Captain Cook was slain right there.

The cattle had been driven down a long, steep trail to the bay the day before the S.S.Humu'ula arrived to pick them up to be sent to the Honolulu market.

Along with Johnny Greenwell, a nephew from O'ahu, we were given battery-operated electric prods and sat at the top of a long chute which led to a heavy plank that jutted out over the water. We would poke the cattle on the behind so they wouldn't change their minds about going into the water.

Some of the cattle made almost olympic dives while others made big belly-flops into the water, a hilarious time for kids. Sailors from the S.S. Humu'ula, in lifeboats, would find a bobbing head, lasso it around the horns and make it fast to the side of the lifeboat. They would then row out to the ship with about three head of cattle on each side. Alongside the Humu'ula a belly strap was placed around the steer. Dripping water and what have you, it was hoisted onto the ship and lowered into the waiting arms of a sailor.

Phew, what kind of work was that?

PROFESSIONAL MANAGERS - "THE BIG FIVE"

The Big Five were the primary agencies in Hawai'i which controlled the sugar industry and just about everything else. These were: Alexander & Baldwin, C. Brewer and Company, Castle & Cooke, Theo. H. Davies and Company, and American Factors (AMFAC - formerly J. Hackfeld & Company)

My uncle George Rodiek's aunt was married to Johann Hackfeld, and so my uncle managed Hackfeld & Co. until the United States entered World War I. Castle & Cooke had a professional manager, Ed. Tenney. It is about Mr. Tenney that I write.

In the '20's, with my father, I used to visit the Tenney home on the ewa corner, mauka of Pensacola Street and Wilder Avenue. It was a big white home, with one of the very few paved tennis courts in Hawai'i in the back. Mr. Tenney was married to a McKee, and so the court may have been the result of the young McKee girls having played lawn tennis at 'Ulupalakua Ranch on Maui, which Capt. McKee owned for a time.

When I knew Mr. Tenney, he was a little old man with dark glasses and a cane. He could not see too well, but as Rose Higgins, telephone operator at Castle & Cooke, told me many years later, "He may have had poor eyesight, but he could always find a girl's fanny to pinch."

He certainly was a leader of The Big Five, or perhaps I should say "Big Four," as Theo. H. Davies, Ltd. was a British-owned firm, and remained quite independent. I suppose they were still smarting over the failure of Britain to take over the Sandwich Islands in the early 1800's.

The first of two stories is about how the Bank of Hawai'i was born. Plantation laborers in the early days were paid in cash, each week, on Saturday. The Bishop Bank, which became First Hawaiian Bank many years later, provided the cash for The Big Five payrolls. Someone at Castle & Cooke goofed and forgot to pick up the payroll before the bank closed one Saturday. Mr. Tenney phoned the president of Bishop Bank and asked that he open up so Castle & Cooke could withdraw money for the payroll. The head of Bishop Bank refused.

On Monday morning the presidents of the sugar agencies got together and formed a new bank, naming it Bank of Hawai'i. This was on the 11th of December 1897.

The second story is about the real birth of Matson Navigation Company. Up until about the middle of World War I, most of Hawai'i's sugar was shipped to California aboard vessels belonging to the American Hawaiian Steamship Company. When carrying goods to war-torn Europe became a more lucrative trade than carrying sugar, American-Hawaiian left Hawai'i and its sugar stranded.

When this happened, Ed Tenney said, "American-Hawaiian will never carry a drop of Hawaiian sugar again," and they never did. Four of The Big Five then put money into the tiny Matson Navigation Company as well as in an oil company named Honolulu Oil. This provided security against Hawai'i's isolation in the future.

Theo. H. Davies, a hard-nosed Brit to the end, tried to stick with American-Hawaiian. But since American-Hawaiian did not visit Hawai'i any more, they switched their allegiance to Waterman Lines and a quota of sugar equal to their share in the Hawai'i sugar industry moved to the mainland on Waterman ships. Davies did not leave the Bishop Bank, either.

Tragedies (Age 8 to 13)

Tragedies, like earthquakes that happen in a small town, leave their mark on you. When I was growing up there were five of these tragedies which I still think about sometimes.

The first was when a playmate and his brother were axed to death by their father, who then turned a gun on himself. Why this person did this horrible thing, I don't know. He did not kill his wife or daughter, however.

The next unhappy happening was when a good friend's house burned down. The family lost all of their possessions. People like my mother quickly got clothes together, including some of mine, for this poor family. My friend Billy Walsh and his mom came over to our house to thank us for our generosity. It was almost a ceremonial occasion. I believe this embarrassed Billy very much, as we were never friends again, or even acquaintances.

Gil Jameson's house was a little over a block away from ours when he was kidnapped and murdered by a Japanese man. I was in the third grade at Punahou and Gil was in the fourth. School mornings, we would assemble in the old Bishop hall corridors by class, once counted (I guess), we marched into our classes. As we were standing there in line, I saw Gil leave with a Japanese man dressed in a white shirt, pants, and wearing dark glasses. Later that day we heard that the man was an ambulance driver, who said that he had come to pick up Gil Jameson to take him to Queens Hospital, as his mother had been seriously injured in an accident.

Later, of course, it was learned that Gil had been kidnapped. In the neighborhood, we guys would walk slowly by the Jameson house with a sort of scary feeling inside. One day, as I was walking by their home, I saw the same man who had taken Gil from school driving slowly by the Jameson's in a Model T Ford. He had on the same white clothes and dark glasses. I ran home and told my parents about sighting the kidnapper, but they wouldn't believe me. It probably would not have helped anyway, as shortly thereafter, they found Gil's body and apprehended the man.

The reason for this tragedy was that the man felt his father had been mistreated by the Bank of Hawai'i on a loan. Mr. Jameson was an officer of the bank but had no connection at all with the loan. The man was hanged. Gil was the Jamesons' only child.

Nowadays the schools are big on sex education, the use of condoms and such, but one thing they didn't condition us about in the old days was epilepsy. My first exposure to this was in the fifth grade at Punahou.

Ralph was one of our friends in class, and one day while taking our required naps on our mats on the floor, Ralph started kicking his legs, flapping his arms and foaming at the mouth. The teacher, not knowing what to do, rushed out of the classroom for help. We kids were scared. I remember I thought of hydrophobia (rabies).

This episode left the class with a repulsive feeling toward Ralph, so we avoided him like the plague. Ralph changed schools and that was the last we saw of him. I often think of how our lack of understanding, brought about by our ignorance, must have harmed Ralph.

The biggest tragedy, if you can call it that, was the sensational Massey case. The Masseys lived just around the corner from our house in Mānoa, and this made it all the more exciting. I was about 12 or 13 at the time, and once, Roger Monsarrat and I had been offered the 'snow' that came from Mrs. Massey's defrosting Frigidaire. Big deal!

In a nutshell, this is the saga:

Lt. Massey (USN) and his wife, along with Navy friends, were at a party in a restaurant located about where the Hotel 'Ilikai is today. Mrs. Massey had an argument with her husband and left the restaurant walking toward Kalakaua Avenue, where she was picked up by five Hawaiian youths, who did sport with her.

Later, Mrs. Massey claimed rape and somehow the police were able to apprehend the five local boys. The entire city, both civilians and military, were outraged. Many taking sides through violent action and brawls. Local Hawaiians, including many old-timers, believed that Mrs. Massey had offered herself up on a silver platter to the locals. The military, of course, felt otherwise. The militia were on standby in case of an uprising on either side.

There was a trial but the accused were let out on bail. During the trail, one day after a court session, one of the five, a Hawaiian named Ka'ahawai, was grabbed by the Masseys, a Navy chief, and

Mrs. Fortesque, (Mrs. Massey's mother). They took him to Mrs. Fortesque's house on lower Mānoa Road, put him in a bathtub, and shot him dead. Then, in broad daylight, with shades drawn in Mrs. Fortesque's Buick, they sped from Mānoa Valley out toward Koko Head with Ka'ahawai's body on the floor of the car.

They were caught with the goods by a policeman who became suspicious when he saw the Buick speeding by with its shades down in broad daylight.

Then came the big trial; the Territory of Hawaii vs. Massey, Fortesque and company. The Masseys, through her mother Mrs. Fortesque, were able to secure the services of a famous trial lawyer, Clarence Darrow, to defend them. But fame alone was not enough for the local jury, and Lt. and Mrs. Massey, Mrs. Fortesque and the Navy chief were found guilty.

The Governor of Hawai'i during that time was Sam King, a part Hawaiian and retired U.S. Navy captain. The governor pardoned the guilty after serving 15 minutes of their life sentences in his office.

Many families were torn between local and military sides including my mother, who with many friends both Hawaiian and Navy, played a difficult balancing act.

SPIES? WHO SAID SPIES?

We rode horses over the sand dunes in Kailua and Kalama when I was little. The only house on the mauka side of the beach road was a great big two-story, white house that belonged to a Mr. Hans Zimmerman.

There was a story about the Zimmerman house told to us young squirts that we believed. Mr. Zimmerman was supposedly caught spying for the Germans in World War I. We could certainly understand that since the house had a lot of long antennae sticking out of the roof. We always gave the place a wide berth, as it was dark and spooky around there. We never ever saw anyone in the yard, even when we peeked.

After World War II started I was told Zimmerman was up to his old tricks and had been caught spying for both Japan and Germany!

The Qwock Hin Family Rice Business

Rice growing on O'ahu died out in the late '20s and one of the last producers to go was the O'ahu Rice Company. The Qwock family owned O'ahu Rice Co. and cultivated rice in paddies on Bishop Estate land on the mauka side of North King Street near the Bishop Museum. Once, when they could not meet their lease rent my father, a Bishop Estate Trustee, arranged to have their rent postponed. Who says the Bishop Estate has no heart?

Hold On!

One day we took our new Airedale dog down to Dr. Katsunuma for his distemper shots. We drove down in our four-door Hupmobile touring car with the open sides.

The dog and I were in the back seat and my mom and dad were in the front seat. A long leash was attached to the dog's collar.

"Under no circumstances are you to let go of that leash," Dad said as we drove out of the driveway. The dog and I looked at each other and I knew that the Airedale was thinking, 'no way will that little twerp hold onto me.' So I wound my end of the leash around the lap-robe rack located on the back of the front seat and sat on the edge of my seat hoping tragedy would not strike before we reached Dr. Katsunuma's house and veterinary clinic. We had not gone very far when whoops, out of the car jumped the Airedale. I would have sailed out with him had the leash not been wound around the lap-robe rack. In stunned silence I hung onto the leash with the dog on the other end until finally my father looked back and saw that the dog, with the leash still attached to his collar, was not keeping up with the Hupmobile.

"I told you to hang onto that dog," dear-old Dad angrily exclaimed. I did not think it too smart to tell him that he had said "leash," not "dog," so I kept quiet except for the tears. A wounded Airedale, now quite respectful, was picked up off the street and again put back with me. Dad tied the leash up short to the lap-robe rack and we proceeded on to the vet. The bill from Dr. Katsunuma was somewhat larger than expected, and to this day, I don't like Airedales.

Uncle Jay's Gift: A Robber Baron Visits Kailua, O'ahu 1925

The McGrew house at Kailua, right on the beach, was a nice place for the younger set to visit in the old days. Besides the super-sandy beach and beautiful blue ocean to swim in, the McGrews had a fenced-in, paved, tennis court. There was a small shaded pavilion next to the court where we used to sit and sip lemonade after whacking the tennis ball around a bit.

The tennis balls were made of hollow white rubber and were smooth on the outside. The racquet frames were steel and strung with stainless steel wire. The net was also heavy steel. Although a lot of fun, we were pilau (junk) players in those days.

Mrs. McGrew had flowing red hair and was considered very beautiful according to my parents and others. "Uncle Reynold" McGrew was a little guy who owned the Siberling Tire Company on Queen Street, just Waikīkī-side of Richards Street in downtown Honolulu. We always got our tires there.

I overheard my mother say Margaret McGrew had been a good friend of Jay Gould. Once, when he was staying with the McGrews in Kailua, I was dragged over to their house to meet this colossal magnate who was a leading member of the railroad consortium rumored to be "ruling" the United States in those days.

"Uncle Jay" was very fat and and wearing a three-piece suit with a heavy gold chain drooping across his vest. He was sitting like a king with one foot up on a footstool because he had 'the gout.' My mother, perhaps thinking that some of Mr. Gould's wealth would rub off on me, insisted that I sit on Uncle Jay's lap.

I sensed that this great baron did not like children, let alone me. Luckily, since his 'ōpū (stomach) was so large, and because he was afraid I would bang into his sore foot, I only had to suffer the indignity of sitting on his lap for about two seconds.

For a long time afterwards I wondered if 'baron' was some kind of royalty we had in America.

Johnny Nash Brings in Tourist Dollars

Johnny and I were pals and we went around a lot together. I remember the time we did our bit for the Hawai'i tourist industry.

It was just another day, so we thought we would meet some of the guys for a swim up at the cement pond. This swimming hole was quite wide and deep and, with care, you could slide down an algae-covered waterfall into the pond from above. However, on our way up to the cement pond, past the dairy and Mānoa Market, the stream ran close by the road at one place below the pond where it formed a shallow pool. So, to cool off a bit, Johnny and I took our clothes off and rolled around in the water.

After a while we discovered some nice oozy mud, and naturally we had a mud fight. Pretty soon we were completely covered with the stuff so we stood up and waved at the people going by.

It was probably erroneous, but we assumed that most of the people were haole (white) tourists and thought they would be pleased to see two 'natives' in the raw.

Moana Hotel Swimming Suits

After taking swimming lessons at the Uluniu Women's Club at Waikīkī from Olympic star, Morikan Weslau, I graduated to the Moana Hotel for surfing and outrigger canoe lessons from David Kahanamoku, Duke's oldest brother.

First, we would check out a gray, one-piece bathing suit with two red stripes around the bottom – hopefully not too baggy or too tight – then to our lockers to change before carrying out heavy 10-foot redwood surfboards for our lesson. We started with limbering-up exercises on the beach and then some basic paddling lessons in the water close to the beach. David would have us paddle out with him way past the Moana Hotel pier, which is no longer there, to where the waves were. He would then push us so that we could catch a wave. This shove by David was necessary because, by the time we got out to the waves, we were too pooped to catch one on our own.

I forgot to mention that "men" in the Moana suits left one shoulder strap unbuttoned. This way you could not only tell the boys from the girls but you could also keep track of your locker key, which was attached with a safety pin from the bottom hole on the loose shoulder strap. I don't know where the girls kept their keys. Catching waves in a canoe was heaven, but the lessons weren't too exciting, so I won't go into that.

Horse Racing and Baseball Caps

In 1877, King Kalakaua turned over Kapiolani Park on O'ahu to the people of Hawai'i for their recreation and enjoyment. This included horse racing. I am told my uncle, George Rodiek, had a string of six racing ponies and the betting was very heavy in those good-old days.

While horse racing at Kapiolani Park was pau (finished) a little before my time, I remember going to the polo matches at Kapiolani Park in the '20's with my parents in our 4-door Hupmobile. There was great excitement with the automobiles lined up on both sides of the huge polo field and, depending on which team you were rooting for, a tremendous honking of horns took place whenever a goal was made.

My enjoyment of polo at Kapiolani Park was really limited to the chocolate-covered ice cream baseballs my dad would buy. These balls were wrapped in tin foil - no stick to hold onto or anything. The fun ended at cleanup time with my mom's saliva-dampened linen handkerchief rubbed hard on my face.

WHEELER FIELD, O'AHU

When I was a little boy, I remember my parents taking me to the Army Air Corps at Wheeler Field in Wahiawa on two occasions; once was to attend a polo match between the Army and the O'ahu Blues, and the other was for an air show.

There was an Army band on hand for the polo match and the Army "brass" were all dolled up in their tropical white uniforms. I remember the Army's polo team was dressed in white too. Very spectacular.

Major George S. Patton, who became one of our warlords 15 years later, was the best Army player. I think he was a three-goal player at the time. Walter F. Dillingham and Arthur Rice were the top polo players for O'ahu. No, I don't remember who won.

The Dole Air Race in 1928 was held in an attempt to grab the kind of publicity Lindbergh's Atlantic flight to Paris received the year before. The race was described as more difficult than Lindbergh's race because Hawai'i was such a small dot way out there in the Pacific. In spite of the danger of getting lost, quite a number of aircraft entered the race, which began in Oakland, California.

Mom, Dad and I, along with hundreds of spectators, waited anxiously for the planes to land at Wheeler Field. While there, we listened to many rumors about planes crash-landing on Kaua'i and Ni'ihau. I believe one actually did land in the kiawe trees on Molokai. I think it was navigated by Amelia Earhart's navigator (no joke intended – well, not much anyway).

Finally one plane landed, rolled to a stop and we went home. Unfortunately, as it happened, the Dole Air Race did not turn out to be a very important world event, coming as it did right after Lindy's famous flight.

Hawai'i got a lot more notoriety on December 7, 1941.

PLUS FOURS, DICKIES & SAILOR MOKUS

Plus fours are the trousers that some golfers are starting to wear again. Buttoned around your legs just below the knee, they were an embarrassment to those of us who had to wear them to school in the first and second grades.

Worse than that was the little flag of material tucked into the front of boys' shorts that was pulled out when they went to the toilet. When I was a little boy, it wasn't important to me to tuck the material back inside my shorts when I was pau (finished) tinkling. But it was very important to mother: "Georgie, tuck your dickie back in," or "Your dickie's out."

Finally, from about the fourth grade on, practically every boy in the school wore sailor mokus. These were a jean-type pant made out of German cloth and were wide at the bottom like a sailor's. Blue was the standard choice.

Sailor mokus were tailor-made by Linn's, a small store down in Iwilei across from the OR&L train depot. Besides sailor mokus, Linn sold palaka (plaid) shirts and shorts, and blue, tan, and white swimming trunks that had two or three contrasting white, red, or blue stripes down the sides and a watch pocket.

Everything was buttons in those days, and all pants, including swimming trunks, had what we called a watch pocket. You could button down the watch pocket on the swimming trunks so you didn't lose the keys to the car when you went surfing.

I thought Linn was Chinese. Wrong! Not until many years later, when I met him at the Honolulu Rotary Club, did I find out he was one haole (white) buggah.

PŪHI

It is quite thrilling to be underwater in the Atlantis submarine off Kailua-Kona, and see the daring diver play with the large pūhi (eel). But under no circumstances would I do that because I have never known an eel I could trust.

When I was eight or nine years old and used to swim at the salt water Memorial Natatorium at Waikīkī, there was a fellow about my age who dove into the pool and came up out of the water shrieking with a big eel clamped onto his right hand. The eel had his teeth firmly attached to the flesh between the boy's thumb and forefinger. The boy was helped out of the water but there seemed to be no way anybody could get that slimy eel's inverted teeth to let go of his hand. The young chap finally whipped his arm up and down sharply to try to shake it off, and though the eel held on, its weight caused the flesh to rip away leaving a large open gash.

Once Chuck Watson speared a big eel off Lanikai on O'ahu one day. Unfortunately the big fellow slid down, off the spear, and then turned around and attacked him. Chuck was lucky to make it back to Tom Prentices' boat, bitten and bloody. Twenty-seven stitches and a lot of bandaids fixed him up.

The other day Gilbert Damasco. who was getting over a pūhi bite on his right index finger, told me about a record setting 98-pound eel that was caught by a man off Pebble Beach in Hilo.

The person who caught this huge denizen of the deep, drove home with it in his jeep, and kept it overnight in his deep freeze. The next day he took it over to the Lyman Museum and gave it to them to stuff and display. On his way home he was in an automobile accident that totaled the jeep. That same day his father died, his sister choked on a chicken bone, and his girlfriend left him. Talk about bad luck.

And, there is a lady in town (I think she is from Micronesia) who is supposed to have lost her entire left hand to the wrist to a ferocious eel. So let this be a warning to you spear fishermen. Remember to look around for a pūhi before you grab a lobster. Eels and lobsters live together you know.

SOMETHING'S FISHY

We had not learned to chew tobacco yet, but back in grammar school we knew how to chew dried fish like 'ōpelu. In fact, we used to carry a hunk of it around in our back pockets. This was before we began to notice girls, of course!

THE CHINESE GRAVEYARD

The Chinese graveyard was way up Mānoa Valley, just past where they grew carnations for lei, but before you crossed the bridge to go up to Woodlawn. It was very interesting for kids because of the pictures on the tombstones of the people buried there and all of the

Chinese writing.

As young kids we would often see Chinese funeral processions going up Mānoa Hill or along lower Mānoa Road. The first car was usually a Model T Ford carrying a Chinese band. Horns would be squawking and cymbals crashing, followed by a long string of cars bearing family and friends.

Someone in the Model T would be tossing out little pieces of thin, coarse paper with holes in it. You see, the devil had to crawl through each hole before getting to the body. By then, hopefully, the deceased would have already arrived in his second world. Strings of firecrackers were also set off to scare the devil.

We used to hide up near the Chinese graveyard when a funeral was coming, either under the bridge, or in the bushes. We would watch the ceremony, which included leaving Chinese money for taxi fare to heaven and wonderful food items such as roasted pork for the deceased.

The reason I know the food was wonderful is because when all the family and friends had departed from the cemetery, and we saw no one left around, we would sneak over to the new grave and cart off the food.

Frequently though, the Chinese watchman at the cemetery would come rushing out of his cottage and chase us off, screaming what must have been some nasty things from his Chinese vocabulary.

Something else interesting about that area was that, not too well buried under the bridge, were a number of skeletons. Sometimes high water in Mānoa Stream during a storm would wash away the dirt along its banks exposing bones. We thought that perhaps these skeletons were from Chinese who were buried under the bridges, near the cemetery rather than in it, because their families could not afford the cost of a burial.

PRINCESS BERNICE PAUAHI BISHOP

• Born in Honolulu on December 19, 1831

• Daughter of High Chief Abner Paki and Laura Konia, the latter a granddaughter of Kamehameha the Great.

• Educated at the Royal School in Honolulu under Mr. & Mrs. Amos Starr Cooke.

• Married Charles Reed Bishop, June 4, 1850.

• Haleakalā, the Bishop home, was the center of musical, literary and social life of Honolulu.

- Mrs. Bishop refused the throne of Hawai'i but "was so loved that she was crowned."
- As the last of the Kamehameha Dynasty, Mrs. Bishop inherited the crown lands and established the B. P. Bishop Estate for its sole beneficiaries: The Kamehameha Schools.
- Died at Keōua Hale, Honolulu, October 16, 1884.
- Buried in the Royal Mausoleum, Nu'uanu Valley, Honolulu.

"A bright light among her people, her usefulness survives her earthly life."

THE HONORABLE CHARLES REED BISHOP

- Born in Glens Falls, New York, January 25, 1822.
- Arrived in Honolulu October 12, 1846, became a naturalized citizen of the Kingdom of Hawai'i in 1849, and was appointed Collector of Customs the same year.
- Married Princess Bernice Pauahi June 4, 1850.
- Established Hawai'i's first bank in 1858.
- Served as a member or president of the Board of Education under the Kings Kamehameha V, Lunalilo, and Kalākaua.
- In 1860, elected a member of the House of Nobles for life.
- Minister of Foreign Affairs under King Lunalilo.
- Trustee of Punahou School for a quarter of a century and one of its benefactors.
- Co-Founder of The Kamehameha Schools and first chairman of the Board of Trustees of the Bernice P. Bishop Estate.
- Founded and endowed the Bernice P. Bishop Museum in memory of his wife.
- Died in Berkeley, California, June 7, 1915, and buried in the Royal Mausoleum in Honolulu.

"Builder of the state, friend of youth, benefactor of Hawai'i, his ashes rest in the Tomb of the Kamehamehas."

THE BERNICE PAUAHI BISHOP ESTATE & THE KAMEHAMEHA SCHOOLS

The Bernice Pauahi Bishop Estate was an important part of my early life as my father, George Miles Collins, was chief engineer of the Bishop Estate at the time of my birth. Seven years later in 1928, he was named a trustee of the estate. He was a trustee for 28 years and was chairman of the board for 15 years. He then resigned and became a trustee of the Campbell Estate for the remainder of his life.

My dad loved the Hawaiian people and he spoke the language fluently. During his years as trustee, he made it a point to address the Kamehameha graduating classes at their commencement exercise each year in Hawaiian and the school's chaplain, Stephen Desha, would follow the address with the English translation. The Hawaiian language was not a part of the curriculum at the schools in those days.

While my father was chief engineer of the estate, and during his early years as trustee, he helped establish the lease rent for much of the Bishop Estate lands. I was with him on many field trips, and I recall one of his most profound statements regarding the preservation of the Bishop Estate's wealth was, "Remember, never to kill the goose that lays the golden egg." It is interesting to look around at failed businesses today in light of this statement.

For many years the Bishop Estate Trustees were chosen by the Territorial Supreme Court and those who were appointed were considered top leaders in Hawai'i's community. The first trustees were: C. R. Bishop, C. M. Cooke, S. M. Damon, C. M. Hyde and W. O. Smith. As the years passed, however, the Hawai'i Supreme Court Judges were appointed for political reasons. Finally all of them were of the same political persuasion and it became obvious that trustees were appointed to the Bishop Estate, not for their talents, but as a method of paying off party creatures for past favors.

Until the one-party system became our lot after World War II, the trustee's commissions were limited to $50,000 per annum. As soon as it became clear that the estate was a "killing ground" for payola, the commission lid was blown off and, as we have seen, these people took home around $800,000 a year.

Without trying to moralize about what has been a large problem, the following excerpts from Princess Bernice Pauahi Bishop's will may show what she had in mind.

Excerpts From Bernice Pauahi Bishop's Will

"I further direct that the number of my said trustees shall be kept at five; and that vacancies shall be filled by the choice of the majority of the Justices of the Supreme Court, the selection to be made from persons of the Protestant religion.

"I further direct that my said trustees shall not sell any real estate, cattle ranches, or other property, but to continue and manage the same, unless in their opinion a sale may be necessary for the establishment or maintenance of said schools, or for the best interest of my estate.

"...to erect and maintain in the Hawaiian Islands two schools, each for boarding and day scholars, one for boys and one for girls.

"...to provide first and chiefly a good education in the common English branches, and also instruction in morals and in such useful knowledge as may tend to make good and industrious men and women.

"I also direct that my said trustees shall have power to determine to what extent said school shall be industrial, mechanical, or agricultural; and also to determine if tuition shall be charged in any case.

"...to devote a portion of each year's income to the support and education of orphans, and others in indigent circumstances giving the preference to Hawaiians of pure or part aboriginal blood.

"I also give unto my said trustees full power to make all such rules and regulations as they may deem necessary for the government of said schools and to regulate the admission of pupils.

"...the teachers of said schools shall forever be persons of the Protestant religion."

Finally, things became so bad by the end of the 1900's that the trustees, in an attempt to restore their "good names," dropped the Bishop Estate name, and now call themselves Trustees of Kamehameha Schools.

ROYAL LINEAGE

They say the offspring of Hawaiian royalty was traced through the mother, as no one was ever sure who the father was. I wonder if this is true in other royal families. Of course, we shouldn't stop there, should we?

EKI PHIPPS

Before Helen Duryea and her family moved next door to us on Kahawai Street in Mānoa, the British consul lived there. Mr. Phipps was a pale, watery-blue-eyed Brit, and his wife was a gorgeous, dark-haired, Spanish lady. They had three children. The oldest, Conchita, was a reproduction of her mother. Then came another girl, a pretty blonde offshoot of her father, as was the boy, Eki. I used to climb trees, pointed out to me by the blonde daughter, to rob eggs from birds' nests for her collection.

It was a fun place next door, because the Phipps had a meandering koi (carp) pond, which they let Eki and me clean when it got too full of algae. Eki also had a great collection of painted lead soldiers. These came complete with "Charge of the Light Brigade" mounted cavalry, skirted Scottish warriors, Indian troops, and more. He also had some small, but real, cannons that could be fired using gunpowder and miniature cannonballs. We would line up two armies facing each other behind abutments, and then using flints, would fire tiny cannon balls at each others troops.

Conchita married a dashing young Honolulu lawyer by the name of Monty Winn who drove a neat convertible. He died after a few years, and beautiful Conchita then married Guy Lombardo, a famous Canadian bandleader.*

* Bertha Weeks said it was Eddie Duchin, not Lombardo. Conchita was in Bertha's class at Punahou School, so Bertha ought to know.

Mae Carden & Mānoa Games

Mae Carden was the best athlete in our bunch. When you did hand-on-hand up a bat to see who got first choice of the players for our neighborhood baseball games, Mae was always picked first before any of the guys. Cinch home run!

We spent every available afternoon playing some kind of outdoor sport. We faithfully followed along with most sport seasons, (Mae did not play football) with the exception of basketball. The high schools seldom played basketball in those days.

We pole-vaulted and high-jumped in Billy Barnhart's yard. Touch football and soccer were played in public parks and school-yards, with shoes never allowed.

Other games we played were capture the flag, kick the can, steal eggs, and polo on bikes and skates. We built homemade sleds and waxed the runners so we could slide down the dried grass on Punahou Hill just above the school. It rarely rained during daylight hours so indoor things like electric trains were sadly neglected.

We swam in ponds and streams, sometimes catching fresh-water eels, polliwogs, frogs, mosquito fish and catfish. One day someone overheard the girls making plans to swim nude up at cement pond. Several of us guys sneaked up ahead of the girls and hid in the long grass alongside the pond. When the girls were undressed and having a great time jumping up and down in the water, we gave a one, two, three, then jumped up yelling "Surprise!" and "'We see you!"

Funny how long afterwards the girls remembered this harmless little incident.

THE FENCE

When I was quite young, I went to school with a family of haoles who were quite dark-skinned and dark-haired, except for one G., later given the nickname of "Ghost." G. was fairer-skinned than the rest of the family, and had blonde hair. He still had his mother's kind of a "Jay Leno" lower jaw, though. As one is wont to do, I asked my father why was it that the R's were all dark except for G., and he explained that the fence was low around the R's house.

Many years later I remembered, and finally understood what he meant.

OUTRIGGER CANOES

One of the biggest days in my life was when I was given the "okay" to take out one of the Outrigger Canoe Club's two-man koa canoes. It was just like passing a driver's license test. Never mind that I swamped the canoe with almost every wave that I paddled hard to catch. The saltwater shooting up my nose and a few healthy gulps of the ocean water instead of air was like heaven to this local boy.

FISH MONGERS

When I was a little squirt in Kailua, we held two teenage fishermen in very high esteem. We hoped that some day we would be good enough to lay fishnets and swim off Kailua and Mokapu and spear fish or grab lobsters like these fellows did.

I may have their names a little mixed up but I think Arthur Rice, Jr. was one of the two and Mark Robinson, Jr. was the other. They lived next door to each other near the Mōkapu-end of Kalama Beach, which was on the Kāne'ohe-side of Kailua Bay.

The Rice and Robinson homes were on great big pieces of

property that ran from Kaleheo Avenue to the beach. I remember both places quite well. At the Rice's, they had a bunch of peacocks,. and I was always stepping on their gooey kūkae (feces), which stuck between my toes. I rubbed it off with sand resulting in both smelly feet and smelly hands.

The Robinson's home was a big two-story house. My mother, who was sort of a card shark, used to play poker there. Ingie Robinson was in my class at Punahou and was the biggest kid in the fourth grade. However, by the time he was pau (finished) with school, he was the smallest kid in the class.

On weekends, Mark and Arthur used to stop by all of the houses along the beach road selling fish and lobsters they had caught. They came by in a Dodge truck with open sides and a canvas roof to keep the sun off the fish.

There was a scale hanging from one of the cross ribs holding up the roof of the truck, and they first weighed the fish purchased, and then cleaned and filleted it for the buyer. Both fishermen looked as though they had just come out of the ocean – bare feet, swimming trunks and no shirts, with messed-up hair and dried salt gleaming from their shoulders. This of course was a smart marketing effort on their part!

Pacific lobsters (no claws and alive of course) were in the truck along with the fish. We used to touch them with our fingers, which made them unhappy, and they would flap their tails and try to swat us with their long thorny feelers.

When some lobsters were bought, they were put in a bucket or wet gunnysack and carried into the kitchen. A huge pot with very little water was put on to boil. When steam began to flip the lid of the pot, the live lobsters were pushed into the pot and the lid slammed shut, leaving a few feeler ends sticking out of the top.

They did not splash around too long, and in a short time their shells turned a bright red. Ready for kau kau!

The Rice and Robinson boys fished with nets and dove, shooting at fish using spears and strips of automobile inner tubing as a sling tied to a hollow section of bamboo.

One time, when they were out in the ocean fishing, one of the boys accidentally speared the other. The one who was speared survived all right, but I always looked over my shoulder when I went spear fishing with others years later.

Rosa's Gym

The Honolulu Police Station was on Bethel Street and Rosa's Gym was on the backside of the same building. Young gentlemen (in my case, very young) were instructed in the manly art of boxing there.

Every Saturday morning my father dropped off his budding 'Jack Dempsey.' After warming up, we would put on gloves and pair up to go a couple of rounds. I was about 11 and was younger than the rest of the "boxers." But I was big and soft. As a result, I usually found myself flat on my back, looking up at the stars. Finally, I was able to hold my own and every once in a while, someone besides me was able to look up at the stars.

Crack Seed

When you had only a nickel to spend, you went into the store and tried to make up your mind whether to buy a bag of crack seed, whole seed, mango seed or see moi (preserved fruit).

Crack seed was a favorite because it took longer to go through a five-cent bag of it than the others, except for see moi, which took a long time to finish because it was so salty sour. My jaws pucker at the thought of it. The lady in the store would ladle out a chunk of crack seed for you, wiping it into a little paper bag that had a small red star printed on it.

At first you pressed the seed out of the bag into your mouth which kept your fingers from getting sticky. Later you had to dig down for the broken pieces of seed or they would start making holes in the bag. You licked your thumb and index finger after each dive into the bag and kept them very clean this way.

One of the challenges about crack seed was to find, and hold separately in your mouth, the little yellow pia pia, or inner seed, to eat after spitting the other pieces of seed out of your mouth. It tasted bitter but was a welcome variation to the sweet-sour taste of the crack seed.

The last thing you did, when the crack seed was all squeezed out, was to tear off pieces of the bag with your teeth in order to suck off all the sweet goo left on the inside of the paper.

So, to make a long story short – at first you blew (rather than spat) out pieces of crack seed, followed by a series of paper spit balls. Lovely!

Little Remembrances from Long Ago

- Picking guavas to make guava jelly
- Reaching up to get mangos with a long bamboo pole
- Eating sweet-sour tamarind seeds from the tree
- Watching a friend bite into a bitter Chinese plum
- Squirting African Tulip pods at each other
- Following the ice truck to get pieces of ice
- Looking for hot-street tar to chew
- Stepping on a bufo (toad) with your bare foot
- Bee stings, wasp stings, and centipede bites
- Picking a lehua flower to see if it would rain
- Sticking the little white pistil from a hibiscus flower on your nose
- Spitting crack seed shells at each other
- Drying out spitballs for rubber-band sling-shot ammunition
- Offering a friend a piece off of your dried 'ōpelu;
- Being sent to the principal's office

Wimbledon Champion - Elizabeth Ryan

Right after Elizabeth Ryan had won the ladies' championship at Wimbledon for about the third time, she went on tour holding tennis clinics for youngsters in a number of cities in the United States including Honolulu. That was in 1930. I had been trapped by my mother who signed me up for 10 tennis lessons. Miss Ryan gave these lessons on the court at the Royal Hawaiian Hotel. Please note I said court, not courts. Tennis was mostly played by the "upper crust" in those days, and from my point of view, it was worse than the dancing lessons which I had to take.

There were about 20 of us, mostly boys, taking the tennis lessons and I thought of them as sissies. For all I know, they may have hated the lessons as much as I did and thought of me as a sissy. A very embarrassing situation.

The crowning blow came at the conclusion of the 10 lessons, when each student was presented with an Elizabeth Ryan "Signature" racquet. By God, her name was scripted right on the throat of the racquet in baby blue!

I never would play with my Ryan racquet, and at that time, did not believe that tennis was here to stay.

Denison's Nutcracker

After Dick Denison's grandfather, George Denison, got through cracking macadamia nuts with his machine, the only hard thing left to do was to open the sealed glass jar to get at the delicious nuts inside.

Grandfather Denison was the inventor of a nut-cracking system consisting of two graduated rollers that allowed macadamia nuts, rolling along between them, to fall through at just the right place to crack the shell. This process broke the hard shell beautifully, but did not harm the tasty meat inside.

Later on others tried to improve on the Denison nutcracker, experimenting with such modern devices as laser beams and high-pitched sound. An electric tuning fork was tried that worked fine for splitting coconuts but could not be fine-tuned enough to break the macadamia nut shell without breaking the nut inside.

In the early days of Hawai'i's macadamia nut history, a Mr. Van Tassel had a macadamia nut tree farm on the southern slopes of Mount Tantalus on O'ahu. His nuts were marketed both in Hawai'i and on the mainland. A glass jar of Van's nuts was a favorite gift from Hawai'i in the '30's and '40's. Van Tassel's biggest marketing mistake, however, was in not hiring Dick Denison's grandfather to invent a glass jar opener.

Theatres Back Then

I saw my first "talkie" at the Empire Theater on King Street in downtown Honolulu. It supposedly took place in Arizona, but outside of horses, I cannot remember the plot at this stage of the game.

Before talkies, a piano player helped dramatize the moving picture. At the Empire Theater it was safer to sit in the balcony or under the balcony, never exposed on the main floor in front of the balcony, because people in the balcony used those exposed below for target practice.

Later on, after the silent movies passed away, I suppose Consolidated Theaters thought you still should have music, so Don George played the organ before the movie started at the Hawai'i Theater. He then moved to the Princess Theater before going to the Golden Gate Theater in San Francisco. Edwin Sawtelle played the organ at the Princess and then moved to the new Waikīkī Theater when it opened up. I remember they had a gadget that revolved around throwing clouds up on the blue ceiling of the Waikīkī Theater.

Other theaters had interesting features too, besides Mickey Mouse. The Pawaʻa Theater had a tin roof, and when it rained you couldn't hear so well. In fact, one time the rain hit the roof so hard, they gave us passes to come back again. In Kona we had a couple of tin-roof theaters. Same problem with the rain, but with an added feature: rats!

Hā'ena Point

Way back in ancient Hawaiian times, a big battle was fought at Hāʻena on the island of Kauaʻi. Hundreds of warriors were killed on the beach there, and over time, their bodies became covered by the shifting sands.

At times, when stormy winds blow on that side of the island, the sand blows away, revealing the skeletons of the brave fallen warriors.

When Allen Wilcox, Jr. and I were little guys, we went there with his Auntie Ethel Wilcox and my mother. We charged around the beach playing war while the ladies sat in the car and "talked story."

I don't know which one of us found the skeleton. It was high up on the beach almost hidden under some scrub ironwood trees. But what a find for small keiki who had never seen a skeleton before.

We puzzled for a while as to how we could take the whole thing back with us to Hanalei, but since the bones were not connected, we came to the conclusion that maybe just the skull would do.

Allen, being the oldest, took the top part of the skull with the eye holes, and I carried the jaw. Pleased as punch, we scurried up the beach to show our treasure to the ladies in the car. Auntie Ethel, who was Hawaiian, turned white with horror, as did my mom.

"Don't you boys know it's bad luck to move a skeleton!" Auntie Ethel exclaimed, her voice quivering with fright.

Of course we didn't know it was bad luck, but we got the picture quickly after seeing the faces of the two horrified ladies. So, wasting no time, we took the skull back to its owner. Or sort of back to its owner, because being that young, we could not remember the exact spot where we had found the skeleton.

Johnny and the Ecosystem

One day my friend Johnny Nash was pushing a homemade

wooden wheelbarrow, with wheels from an old baby buggy, down Kahawai Street. He was bawling his eyes out, and told me his father had sent him off to get a load of cow manure for the vegetable garden. Very embarrassing for Johnny.

I told Johnny I knew it was a pilau (dirty) thing to have to do, but I would go along with him for moral support. So off we went to the nearby dairy. First of all, though, we had to ride some bucking calves, and I think we went home with more manure on us than in the wheelbarrow. A sad beginning but a happy ending.

Johnny Nash Solves the Balkan Situation

One day Johnny went home crying from a fight. He had a terrible bloody nose, and what was to become a big black eye. His dad's solution to this episode was to send Johnny back out to do battle again with the person with whom he had been fighting, and to have him keep fighting until he won.

Fortunately, he ran into a group of his buddies on the way, and a practical solution to the problem was found. His bigger opponent was convinced that it would be wiser to let Johnny beat him up rather than to have to take on the whole Mānoa Gang.

Kīlauea Lodge nee Camp Westervelt

Having recently spent a relaxing three days at Kīlauea Lodge with old-time friends, I thought I'd tell you what the place is like today, and what it was like a long time ago.

The lodge is just off the main highway on the old Volcano road, about a mile or so toward Hilo from the Volcanoes National Park entrance. The rooms are first class and very comfortable. Those closest to the lodge have fireplaces in them, and bathroom towels are hung on heated towel racks.

Breakfast is all you could ask for, and the dinner menu and service by the lodge staff is excellent. I was most impressed, though, with the handsome hardwood floors in the main lodge dining room, and the beautifully finished koa-wood dining tables.

However, this was not the same YMCA Camp Westervelt I went to in the early '30's. In fact, I believe it was next door to the present lodge that was built for the 'Y' in 1938. At any rate, my current visit brought back nice memories.

I will not tell you about the fun I had almost getting lost in

45

a huge lava tube across the street from our camp, or about roasting marshmallows and weenies under still-hot lava near the footprints. No, I just want to let you know about the camaraderie amongst our group of young whippersnappers as we sat around the campfire at night singing YMCA songs, like Clementine...."Then the Y boys to the rescue, and they arrived there just in time, threw a plank out into the water, and they saved my Clementine."

A Trip to Kīlauea and Keauhou Bay

One summer vacation a group of about 25 of us from Honolulu went to the Big Island on a YMCA camping trip.* Mr. Barnes from Kamehameha Schools and Mr. Cole, Billy Cole's dad, were chaperones and kept us from getting into trouble.

We spent about five days at Camp Westervelt near the Kīlauea volcano, explored everything there, and met Dr. Thomas Jagger, the famous volcanologist.** The Thurston Lava Tube was a real hike in those days – no lights, and still a lot of stalactites and stalagmites.

We also went to Keauhou Bay and stayed at the Reverend Walker's dormitory-type house. Only catchment water (it tasted like the tin roof) and no heater. But all of us still had a great time.

To get to the Keauhou beach area in those days required going to the end of the paved Ali'i Drive, at about where the Keauhou Beach Hotel entrance is today. Then you went over a cattle guard and were on Bishop Estate property. The road was 'a'ā lava chunks (later cinder) all the way to the beach. To get to the houses on the south or Ka'u-side of Keauhou Bay, you had to drive on the black-sand beach, which you didn't do at high tide.

A half dozen or so wooden plank fishing canoes, covered with galvanized tin or coconut branches. were pulled up on the beach. There were no piers, or ramps, or Fairwind catamarans in those days.

Rev. Walker's place was at the peak of a very bare hill between He'eia and Keauhou Bays, and a person had an unobstructed view all around. There were only three or four houses on a short road on the He'eia-side of Keauhou Bay at that time, where some Hawaiian families lived. We watched an old Hawaiian lady, said to be over 100 years old, go in for a swim in her mu'umu'u.

The water in Keauhou Bay back then, before population intrusion, was clean and clear, and the bottom was not full of silt. The limu (seaweed) was good to eat, too.

Some of the boys on the trip were: Roger Monsarrat, Eugene Beneyas, Bob White, Bobby Midkiff, Thurston Twigg-Smith, Charles "Fat" Guard, Roy Vitousek, Jr., Billy Cole and Charlie Judd.

**At an earlier time, Thomas Jagger held me over Halema'uma'u Crater for a look. There was no fence and I hoped Mr. Jagger would not slip or have a heart attack or something.*

A MADGE TENNENT PORTRAIT

Did you ever have to sit for a portrait artist? I don't mean the kind you willingly do when you are an important grownup, but the ones your mother arranged when you were a little person.

I remember once overhearing someone tell my mother, "Gerry, you must have Georgie sit for Madge Tennent. Every child in town is having one of Madge's charcoal portraits done."

What a pain in the neck. First, a hot bath under the supervision of Mom, with the wet soapy washrag rubbing your face raw. Then the clean, charming little suit, and the long drive from Mānoa to Nu'uanu.

In the Madge Tennent studio, thumbs and fingers pushed me into the "proper" position under the hot lights, and I was told to sit still. Right off the bat, I felt something by my left ear I had to scratch or I'd die. Then a little itch on the right side of my nose needed fixing.

Several times after a scratch, Mom would notice an exasperated look on Madge's face, and would hiss at me between clenched teeth, "Sit still."

Madge Tennent's art is highly valued today. Would anyone like to buy my portrait?

EARLY FAMILY RHYMES & POEMS

Oh, I'd rather have eyes than a nose,
I'd rather have fingers than toes,
I'd rather have hair on the top of my head,
Than down where the Wurtzberger flows.

In a parlor a davenport stands,
A couple sitting and holding hands, so far, no farther.
But now in the parlor a cradle stands,

A mother weeping and wringing her hands, so far, no father.

Edith Donaghue McMillin,
Ate her fill of watermelon,
Late that night, with Baron Pruitt,
Edith wet before she knew it!
Moral: "goops that can't control the bladder will
never top the social ladder."

Epitaph:
Here lies my daughter Charlotte,
Born a virgin, died a harlot,
For 12 long years she kept her virginity,
And that's quite a record for this vicinity.

SQUAT TAG

You don't see it any more, but in the '30's I remember passing cars stopped along the roads, with entire families all going to the hale li'i li'i. Dad and the boys would be standing by the right front and rear of the automobile doing their business, and Mama and the girls, also on the right side of the car, squatting down to do their business. I guess you could call it a little bit of local color.

FLEAS IN THE DOGHOUSE

After listening to Jackie tell us about her conquests with boys, I thought I might try some of that. I think she was in the third grade and I was maybe in the fourth.

Seeking a secluded spot, I invited her to join me in our doghouse, which Beau, our cocker spaniel, didn't seem to use any more. She slipped into the house rather easily, and I with much squeezing, followed her.

Almost immediately, I sensed something was wrong. Small, almost infinitesimal, black dots appeared on Jackie's face, arms and legs. I looked at myself and it was a repeat.

We quickly left the doghouse, ladies first of course; and so ended our tryst.

MRS. BARNHART'S HOUSE IN MĀNOA

Mrs. Barnhart's house was like a neighborhood YMCA. We

gathered on her porch and played in her yard a lot. She never said, "Wipe off your muddy feet," and always had lemonade and cookies for us.

We hardly ever saw Mr. Barnhart, though. He would park his car in the garage and sort of slide past us into his bedroom, never to be seen again. I thought it different that he had his own separate bedroom and Mrs. Barnhart had hers. When I grew up, I discovered that other married people sometimes have separate bedrooms, too.

During track season, the Barnhart front yard, about 40 feet wide by 50 feet long, was used for shot put, pole vaulting and high jumping. It rained a lot and the front yard and porch were quagmires. I'd like to say that many of the early "Barnhart athletes" later picked up Olympic gold medals, but I can't.

THE NEIGHBORHOOD DISCOUNT STORE

One of the members of our Mānoa gang perfected the art of pilferage to the point where he had to open a store in his house in order to market his loot.

He used to wear a simulated leather jacket, with an elastic bottom, when he went on his forays in downtown Honolulu. The S.H. Kress store was his major supplier, and he would relieve the store of much of its yoyo, pocket knife, whistle, and flashlight supply. At home his dresser drawers contained much merchandise, marked down of course, and this is where we were able to buy 15-cent yoyos for 10 cents and 25-cent yoyos for 15 cents.

Sometimes walking past Mānoa Market he would ask us what kind of gum we wanted. He would go into the market and relieve its revolving gum machine of some of its Blackjack, Dentine, or Juicy Fruit gum. He was able to buy sincere friendships this way.

The trick I liked best was the way he got free Milk Nickels. These were 5-cent ice cream bars on sticks. One stick in each carton of 12 had the word "Free" stamped on it. He would pull out sticks and push them back in the ice cream bar until he found the "free" one. If you went into the store to buy a Milk Nickel, you always checked the bottom where the stick went into the bar. If the chocolate around the stick was broken, you knew our friend had been there, and you would then look into another box for an untampered-with Milk Nickel bar.

From neighborhood store manager, our talented pilferer went into law enforcement. He became a top detective with the

Honolulu Police Department.
It takes one to catch one.

OBLIGATIONS

You could beg off of many things, but when it was time to pick guavas and mangos for your mother's jelly and chutney making, only a really rotten kid would refuse to help the old lady.

As a matter of fact, we enjoyed these outings very much. Sometimes we would go as a family, and at other times, a group of young friends were sent out with buckets and sacks to pick the not-so-ripe guavas and mangos. When we went out as a group, collecting the fruit always took a lot longer than if you went with just your mother. This was because of the time-outs taken to throw overripe guavas and mangos at each other.

When someone complimented Mom for the wonderful jelly or chutney, it was always nice to hear her say that "Georgie" did most of the work.

LAUHALA

A long time ago, lauhala mats made in Hawai'i, covered the floors of our homes, or at least the living rooms and lanais of our houses at the beach. Hopefully, this art will make a strong comeback if we become a monarchy again!

On O'ahu, walking along beaches in Punalu'u and Kahala and other places where the seas were calm, you would always see bunches of leaves from the hala trees in the water being softened and bleached before being dried and stripped for weaving.

BREEDING HORSES

Before World War II, Parker Ranch bred horses for the United States Cavalry. The ranch improved its own stock, and at the same time, made money by providing an important service for Uncle Sam.

The breeding business was no small operation when you consider the official 1960 agricultural census recorded 17,000 horses at Parker Ranch. And each cowboy had a string of 17 horses, thus, a large number of Hawai'i's horses served our army well on polo fields, in parades, and playing their part in "The Charge of the Light Brigade" type battles the Army played until World War II.

And now to the sexy part of this story: According to Pete L'Orange, who worked for Parker Ranch a number of years ago, donkey teasers were used before purebred studs were introduced to the mares. This was necessary because, until a mare in heat became really interested in procreation, she would frequently flail out with her hind legs trying to kick her suitor into next Tuesday. Breeders could afford to have a jackass booted around, but not a thoroughbred stud worth thousands of dollars. The donkeys, thus employed, were all given vasectomies by Dr. Case, or other Parker Ranch veterinarians, to prevent any mulish slip-ups from occurring in the breeding process.

Finally, when the mare had settled down and was ready for the real thing, the donkey was excused, and her stud was led in and introduced to her by guidons. These guidons were cowboys who assisted the stud in finding the target. "Waste not-want not!"

I wondered why this tortuous way of breeding horses was done, when artificial insemination would have been so much easier. Pete L'Orange replied, "Like a good painting, too many copies from the same stud would bring down the price of colts."

THE JACKASS

A long time ago, when my father was a trustee of the Bishop Estate, he would travel to Hawai'i Island from O'ahu to survey estate lands on Hualālai mountain which were under lease to a number of ranch owners.

I traveled along with him on many of these surveys in the late '20s and early '30s. These trips were done on horseback usually lasting for a couple of weeks. Once however, I missed being in Kona with him on a survey done on the McCandless Ranch which turned out to be one of his more colorful trips.

The survey began as usual at the McCandless store alongside the highway near Mākena. Here, the people going on the trip were fitted out with horses, saddles, bridles, and of course, the long skirted rain slickers that covered both saddle and rider. It rained almost continuously up mauka.

Link McCandless, owner of the ranch, had been Hawai'i's delegate to the U.S. Congress when it was a Territory of the United States. He was also the highest muck-a-muck in the Democratic Party, and was also known as "one hell of a politician".

Knowing something of my father's anatomy, Link had a

fitted saddle made mostly for dad's derriere. With my father comfortably seated, the survey party took off toward the forests that were high up on Hualālai. The group had just closed a gate and was moving into a new pasture when a lonesome jackass, also known as a Kona Nightingale, discovered my father's mount was a mare in heat.

The jackass, moving at a full donkey trot, tried to mount the mare, who objected greatly to the little bugger's advances, bucking and kicking at him. The mare's gyrations almost unseated my father, who was fortunately rescued by the cowboys.

He later said he was more worried about what the jackass might do to him than he was about falling off the horse.

A Big Island Ranch

When I was about 10 years old my father took me with him on a visit to the "P" Ranch, which is at the south end of Kona. We were on horses for about a week covering the ranch. Mr. P, owner of the ranch, was our host. I remember he was a large man with a big black moustache.

One day, way up mauka in the forest, we came to a clearing and stopped by a small house where a lady with several small children came out to greet us. "Daddy, Daddy," the children cried, as they ran up to Mr. P. About two days later we came to another cabin in the woods and some different children came pouring out the door, exclaiming, "Daddy, Daddy!"

My father explained this phenomenon to me later by saying, "It gets cold at night up here in the mountains."

Honolulu's Beaver Grille

The Beaver Grille was a favorite restaurant below Merchant on Fort Street in Honolulu. It was really called the "Merchants' Grille," although there was a gold-painted replica of a beaver on the sign over the marquee. In the early days after World War II, businessmen crowded the place for stew, frankfurters and that sort of male fare.

I think the establishment was owned by a relative of the Lycurgus', and before the war my parents took me there a couple of times for frog-leg dinners, which were served in a banquet room upstairs in the restaurant. I still can't face frog legs, but I do remember you could get a good view of the golden beaver from the windows upstairs.

Sea Sled Racing – 1932

Elbridge Durant lived in Mānoa when I was a little kid and at one time had become interested in sea-sled racing.

A sea sled was a flat plywood boat, about six-feet long and four-feet wide all the way from the stern to the bow. The bow curved up from the bottom of the boat and fastened to a top deck that extended back about three feet to the cockpit. The transom was reinforced with another thickness of plywood. A 25-horse-power Johnson motor, with a gas tank surrounding the flywheel, powered the thing.

We helped, or I should say watched, Elbridge glue and screw the boat together. The curve on the piece of plywood for the bow was made by steaming it over a water-filled brass laundry tub which rested on top of a gas stove. Very interesting.

Finally, the day for a tryout arrived. We all went down for the launching. The motor was so heavy it would have sunk the boat, so someone held down the bow when the boat was in the water. After many pulls on the starter cord, plus fiddling with the spark, choke, and other gadgets on the motor, it started. Elbridge quickly lay forward on the bow, and with the steering arm extension with its built-in throttle in hand, gave her the gun. Fortunately our buddy, who had been holding the bow down, darted to one side as the sea sled roared out over the passive water in Honolulu Harbor.

One minute later the motor died and Elbridge leaned all of his weight on the bow of the boat so it wouldn't sink. We rowed out and towed the boat, and its builder, back to shore.

Frankly, this exposure to outboard motor racing was enough for me. Surfing and fishing were more to my liking.

King Kamehameha's Cave

Way up on the south side of Mānoa Valley, above Hart Woods' house in Woodlawn, was a fairly large cave. Naturally, we gave it the name of "Kamehameha." There must be lots of caves in Hawai'i with that name.

During the '20's and early '30's, without TV, or even radio that was worth much in those days, we would sometimes go on a hike for something fun to do. There were two relatively short hikes we took. One was to this cave, the other through the thick bamboo to Mānoa

Falls. The falls were a four-hour hike and King Kamehameha's cave was about a two-hour hike.

The cave was very spooky because there was a lot of evidence of human habitation in it. Clothes, empty cans, Chinese ceremonial candles (probably stolen from the Chinese cemetery nearby), and animal bones scattered about. Whenever someone escaped from prison, we were sure he was holed up in Kamehameha's Cave.

Only the bravest of us lads poked his nose in the cave first. I usually volunteered to protect our rear from sudden attack.

BUMBLE BEES, HONEY BEES AND CENTIPEDES

Bumble bees liked to make their homes in wooden telephone poles. When things were slow in our Mānoa neighborhood, we would find a bumble bee hole in a telephone pole and put the mouth of a glass jar over it. Then we would hit the telephone pole vigorously on the opposite side and watch for the big black bumble bee to back into the jar.

After catching one, you put holes in the top of the jar so the bee could breathe and he would buzz away in the jar for quite a while. Queen bumblebees were white and a rare treasure!

A great game to play with honey bees is done with a can of spray ether and some thread. First you knock out a couple of bees with ether, then tie the bees with an arm's length of thread. When the bees shake their little heads and come to, (while still holding on to the end of the thread) you try to get your bee to attack your friend rather than you, while he tries to get his bee to sting you. With centipedes it's a different story.

I never knew which end was the business-end of a centipede, so I never played around with them. One of my classmates in the fifth grade had one as a pet. He was a sneaky guy, so I did not put any faith in his instructions on how to defang a centipede.

MADAM WEISBERG AND WANDA LEE BENOIT

During my years in elementary school at Punahou, my father used to drive me to school early in the morning, at about 6:30am. This allowed me to participate in pre-school activities like touch football. At 8am, when matriculation began, my athletic friends and I would sit down in class all sweaty, sticky, and smelly.

I hated driving to school with the old man, because all the

way down I was drilled on the multiplication tables, plus math problems such as, "What is 219 plus 89, minus 42?" Tough problems like, "If John had 92 chickens and Mary had 69, and every other day each chicken laid one egg, how many roosters were there?" Sometimes it was Latin declensions, with questions like, "What is the present, past and future of the verb "to make?" Answered Georgie, "facio, facere, fece, factus."

The only relief I got from this early morning tutoring ordeal was when we were flagged down for a ride by Madam Weisberg, or drove past Wanda Lee Benoit. Madame Weisberg, who had been my third grade French teacher, used to stand in the middle of the road frantically flapping her wings. If you didn't stop, you ran over her. I would squeeze over, Madam Weisberg would crowd into the front seat next to me, and she and Dad would start speaking animatedly in German. She sprayed quite a bit when she talked, and I think she believed in only Saturday night baths. During third grade French class, she used to bend over, close to my left ear, to try to help me pronounce my French. I did not learn much French but I do remember how wet my ear got.

Wanda Lee Benoit was another matter. She and her family lived near us in the same house Lieutenant and Mrs. Massey, of the famous Massey case, later lived. Sometimes on our way to school, there would be delightful, beautiful, Wanda Lee Benoit. She carried her books in her right arm and walked the curb perfectly with one foot placed directly ahead of the other. You can imagine what this performance did to her hips. Around and swish up on one side, around and swish up on the other.

Good old Dad's attention would be completely diverted by this scene. After barely missing the curb on the opposite side of the street, or perhaps a telephone pole or two, he would be silent for the rest of the way to school.

LANIKAI AND THE MID-PACIFIC COUNTRY CLUB

Lanikai is a beautiful strip of beach land between Kailua and Waimānalo on windward Oʻahu. You enter and leave Lanikai on the Kailua side via a road that takes you past a fake lighthouse on the beach-side and Poulison's unpainted, weathered house on the other. The Poulison house looked like it had fallen from the sky, and been impaled by a sharp outcropping of rocks piercing the home right in the middle of the living room.

The one-way road on the mauka side is called A'alapapa. At the Waimanlo end, A'alapapa becomes Mokulua Drive, which is the road closest to the beach, and will take you back out past the 'lighthouse' to Kailua. A lovely subdivision there was developed by Charles R. Frazier*, a Honolulu realtor, who had come to Hawai'i to set up the billboard sign business for Foster and Kleiser.

Quite a number of Scotsmen had beach houses at Lanikai, with the only thing missing to make their weekends happy and complete, was a local golf course.

Just the other side of Lanikai, off a low place in the hill off A'alapapa Street, was some land that sloped into Kawainui Swamp. Frazier and his friends found the land belonged to the Bishop Estate. They were able to arrange a suitable lease, and developed a nine-hole golf course.

The clubhouse was very frugal at first, with not much more than a small bar, a hikie'e (large Hawaiian couch), and a couple of card tables with chairs. Mr. McKay (pronounced McKey) was the club's pro who lived with his family in a tiny house close to the clubhouse.

While the burrs in the grass exceeded the burrs heard in the clubhouse, I'd say that at least 50 percent of the early members were of Scottish origin.

So, it was that my non-Scottish father decided to take up golf. After all, the new golf club was situated on Bishop Estate land and my father was a trustee of the estate. What he had most in common with these heather-bred guys was that he did not like to part with a quarter without a very good reason. Therefore, I became his caddy and had to keep my eye on every ball he hit. I went around barefoot in those days and the burrs that stuck to my tough feet were nothing, but the sharp thorns from the male kiawe trees were no fun at all.

Dad often played golf with Kelly Henshaw, Bob McCorriston, and Peter McLean. I used to watch in awe when Kelly Henshaw teed off on the first hole. He would face the clubhouse and with the green over his right shoulder (he was left handed), he would wind up and give the ball a heck of a swat sending it in a huge arc of about 180 degrees. The ball would somehow drop down on the fairway in perfect line with the green, ready for Kelly's next controlled hook, which would send it soaring toward the hole.

One day, my Dad and I were playing as a twosome together, although I was still required to know where his ball landed. When he sunk a hole-in-one on a par-three hole he said, "For gosh sakes, don't tell anybody I made a hole-in-one or I'll have to buy drinks for the whole place." I speechlessly indicated I would keep mum about it.

We gave a friendly greeting to some golfers on an opposite fairway without breathing a word about the hole-in-one. Upon arriving back at the clubhouse a couple of hours later, we found the parking lot was filled to overflowing with cars and male golfers, most of them Scots. They were crowded into the clubhouse, elbow to elbow, shouting congratulations to father and thanking him for the drinks.

I think there was insurance you could buy to cover excessive bar tabs resulting from holes-in-one, but my dad didn't dream he would ever get one. So, you see, insurance does have its place after all!

Pressure from the Honolulu Outdoor Circle resulted in Frazier changing his occupation from an outdoor sign mogul to a real estate mogul.

PARKING IN DOWNTOWN HONOLULU

The Fort and King Streets intersection was the busiest one in town in the days before electric traffic signs. Liberty House and the two McInerney stores were there along with many other businesses up and down the sides of each street.

Policemen in "sensible" khaki uniforms sat in little khaki-draped cubicles about waist high. A khaki-colored umbrella was provided for rain and shade. Extending out of the top of the umbrella was a hand-operated "stop" and "go" sign on a swivel, which was used by the cop to direct the flow of traffic.

My mother was not a very good driver, and about the last thing she could do was back into a parking place. When she went shopping downtown, she would double-park near Fort and King Streets and wave at the policeman in the center of the intersection. He would fold up his "stop" and "go" sign, come over, and park her car.

Mom got this special service because she knew all the cops. Off duty, they played Hawaiian music at most of the parties in town. Some nights they would drop by our house after parties and serenade us. My parents would invite them in for a few drinks of 'ōkolehao (Hawaiian whiskey) and a couple of songs. This was during prohibition.

THE HALLOWEEN STASH

Sixty-five years ago, "Trick or Treat" just meant "Trick." One nasty, little Halloween trick we played involved boxes. There were no garbage cans in those days, just garbage boxes. On the neighborhood roads, hidden just around corners where unsuspecting automobile drivers could not see them, we built garbage box barricades.

Cars would come to screeching stops just before crashing into the wooden boxes, and angry drivers would hop out of their cars and throw the boxes aside. The Mānoa Gang, hiding out behind hedges, would then pelt the drivers with rotten eggs and run off as fast as our legs could carry us, laughing all the way. Nasty little hoodlums we were.

About three weeks before Halloween, we started collecting ammunition for our forays. This "stash" was primarily made up of tomatoes and chicken eggs. Only a few of the latter, though, because they would be missed out of the icebox. It was different in Johnny's case, because he had real live chickens at his house.

One time though, we overdid it with Johnny's eggs. For a whole week we took eggs from nests and from under chickens. Often you knew an egg was available when a chicken gave a big "bagawk!" Anyway, we stopped swiping the eggs when Norman, Johnny's dad, said to Johnny's mom, "If those chickens don't start laying eggs, there are going to be a lot of birds on the barbie!"

ETHNIC CLEANSING

In elementary and junior high schools on O'ahu, the closest we came to giving minorities a bad time was when the Army and Navy "brats," as we called them, piled out of the big gray and green buses at the first of the school year.

A lot of these kids, along with their parents, were new arrivals to Hawai'i. My goodness what white legs and pretty shoes! The rest of us were made up of many different nationalities, but even the haoles had tans and tough feet.

In athletic games like soccer, football, and baseball, no shoes were allowed, so right off the bat the military kids were persecuted.

Usually by the second year, the Army and Navy guys had tough feet and tans, so they became "members of the club."

Maggie's Inn

A long time ago on Ala Moana Boulevard, close to the Honolulu waterfront, was a drive-in called Maggie's Inn. Following the repeal of prohibition, Maggie's was one of the first establishments in town to secure a "dispenser general" (booze) license.

At that time, our bunch of guys in Mānoa Valley were quite young, between the ages of 10 and 15. We had all heard from our parents how President Roosevelt was ruining the country, but wondered why he was so bad if they could now buy liquor at liquor stores and hotels instead of bootleggers.

Someone got the bright idea that we ought to see if we could buy a drink. So one night, after a little careful planning, we borrowed hats from our fathers, brought pillows from home to sit on, and talked a girl in our neighborhood named Helen into letting us borrow her family car after her father and mother went to sleep.

Although most of us knew how to drive, none of us had licenses. After her parents were asleep, Helen shinnied down a wili-wili tree* from the second floor of her house, and we silently rolled the family's Buick down the driveway. We started the engine and drove down to Maggie's Inn sitting on pillows, our hats pulled down, and with double chins to make us look at least 20 years older.

At Maggie's Inn we tooted the horn for service and when the waitress came to the car she asked, "Eh, you kids old enough for drink?" With our voices lowered we assured her we were old enough and ordered rum and cokes. No problem!

After our big challenge to society, we drove back to Mānoa and gunned the car so it had enough speed to make it up into Helen's garage without waking her parents.

Wiliwili trees are very thorny, but Helen had been up and down the tree so many times the thorns were worn off.

Baseball Greats Visit Hawai'i

Bill Cartwright, the founder of American baseball, is buried in Nu'uanu Cemetery on O'ahu. Japanese tourists frequently visit the site with their cameras to take photos of the headstone marking his grave.

About 1926, my mother and I returned to Honolulu on the Dollar Lines' President Tyler after visiting relatives in San Francisco.

I don't know why it was that we did not come back on a socially acceptable Matson ship, but anyway, a few of us traitors got off this round-the-world ship in Honolulu.

A baseball team headed by Ty Cobb, which was on its way to exhibition games in Japan, was with us on the trip. Before getting off the Tyler I was given a real live baseball that had been signed by all of the members of the team!

My Uncle Kelly ("Slide, Kelly! Slide!") told me Ty Cobb was a real dirty baseball player, and he even sharpened the cleats on his shoes so they were razor sharp. This was so when he slid into bases or at home plate on close calls, he could slide in feet first, giving opponents second thoughts about tagging him out.

Another great event to hit Hawai'i's shores, besides the Depression in the early '30's, was a visit by the "King of Swat," Babe Ruth. Boy, he sure filled up the old Honolulu stadium in Mo'ili'ili.

By then, the Babe couldn't run too well, so he just stood at the plate and hit home run after home run into the stands. What power. As each ball soared up into the atmosphere, hundreds of kids tried to guess where it would land, and scrambled over each other fighting to get balls as they landed in the crowd.

At the end of this marvelous exhibition, it was announced that Babe Ruth would sign the baseballs he had swatted into the stands. A whole bunch of sweaty youngsters, some bleeding, some with torn shirts, each with his ball, were herded into a long line by stadium ushers for the signing.

I was bloody, and my shirt was torn, but I didn't have a baseball.

MŌKAPU

When I was in my teens my favorite body surfing spot was at Mōkapu on O'ahu. If we went by Koko Head, we would usually stop on the way back to Honolulu, to body surf some more at Mōkapu when the waves were good.

On other occasions we would return home over the Old Pali Road and have green-guava fights between cars along the way. Model A's could make it up the Pali from windward O'ahu easily, but sometimes we were in Model T's, and had to drive via Koko Head, as a Model T couldn't make the Pali except in reverse gear. (Reverse was the most powerful gear in a Model T.)

Besides the surf, Mōkapu had other attractions too. One

thing was the gooney birds that made their nests in the low wind-blown sea grape trees. These ground-nesting birds learned to lay their eggs in the trees after donating several generations of offspring to the mongoose that were plentiful there. The gooneys seem to almost crash when taking off. They are big, clumsy birds.

The Mōkapu Yacht Club on the Kāne'ohe-side of Mōkapu was a nice place to hang out. It was pretty shallow on the Kāne'ohe Bay side, so all the sailboats had center boards. The girls sailed moon boats and tipped over a lot. We used to try to rescue them and they liked that. Many appeared to tip over on purpose.

Sometimes we would pick up long, ugly, red worms from the silt-laden bottom of the bay by the Yacht Club and throw them at each other. If you swung them around your head carefully so the guts didn't whoosh out too soon, the centrifugal force would build up, and you could get a lot of distance with your throw toward the other person. This sport was not enjoyed by very many of the girls.

THE PINEAPPLE CANNERIES

Next to sugar, pineapples provided the most jobs and income for Hawai'i while I was growing up. The Dole, Libby and Del Monte companies hired many of us for the summer harvesting months.

Freshly picked pineapples from the fields were transported in large crates on OR&L Railroad flatcars, or by truck, to the various canneries. There, muscular men manhandled the crates from the unloading platform and the pineapple was fed into the Ginaca machines.

An engineer who worked for Dole invented the Ginaca machine. This machine removed the outside skin of the pineapple and cored it in one motion. From the machines, the pineapples flowed out in an assembly line operation for final trimming of "eyes," and were automatically shunted to machines that sliced them for various-sized cans.

The trimming operation was interesting at times. Women of every ethnic origin imaginable worked along conveyor belts trimming the pineapples with razor-sharp, slightly curved butcher knives. A man at the end of the line sharpened the knives for the girls. Every now and then, one lady would get angry with another one, and they would go at it with their sharp knives. Police whistles would blow, and security guards and matrons would come running. Not good to have blood in the pineapple!

Syrup was automatically added to the pineapple in the cans, lids were placed on the cans, which were sealed, and the cans revolved into the cookers. After cooking, the cans were loaded and stacked onto wooden racks. A forklift driver moved the load into the cooling room. When the bright cans had cooled they were either labeled, cased for shipment, or stacked in large piles for later labeling and casing. The men doing can stacking were paid piecework in those days so teams of men would stack them working at a furious pace, almost a blur of movement.

I worked for three months driving a forklift for Libby, McNeill, Libby down at Ewilei during the summer of 1938. I worked 12 hours per day, seven days each week, and was paid 37 cents per hour. Overtime at time-and-a-half was paid after eight hours. That summer I earned enough money to buy my first car, "Jezebel," a Model A Ford. I went back and forth to school in it that year.

Because we were assigned to keep the stacked cans of pineapple moving from the cookers to the cooling room, we were given only 15 minutes for a meal. We drivers felt like big shots because we did not have to stand in line for our food. What else, with just 15 minutes? Usually the fare was beef stew and rice, two tall glasses of syrupy iced tea, and six slices of buttered bread. Special price for us was 25 cents.

The only noteworthy thing that happened that summer was when I jumped off the forklift at the last moment to go to the toilet. With my mind only on peeing, I unwittingly dashed into the ladies' toilet. Whistles blew, girls screamed, and for about one minute I thought I'd had it. A smile, an apology, and a quick dash from girl's room to boy's room, and I was off the hook without spilling a drop.

OUR MILK COMES FROM CONTENTED COWS

There were a lot of independent dairies in the old days. My granduncle, Paul Neumann, was supposed to have had one on the slopes of Makiki on O'ahu. Well before my time, of course. When I was little, C. Montague Cooke had a dairy off upper Mānoa Road, in a pasture just before you get to the Waioli Tea Room. His milk went mostly to members of the Cooke family living in Honolulu.

The Mānoa Gang found the C. Montague Cooke dairy to be a fine place to practice throwing the discus and javelin. Dried cowpies provided good discus material.

Another dairy in Mānoa, run by a Japanese family, was

at the end of Kahawai Street. Next to the road to the dairy was a Japanese language school. This is where I went with the servants to see Japanese movies and bon dances. It was held in the open and everybody had umbrellas because it rained a lot in Mānoa Valley. Still rains a lot in Mānoa Valley.

Locey's Dairy was located in Wai'alae. It was replaced with the Bishop Estate Wai'alae-Kahala housing development a few years after the end of World War II. Residents in the new houses blamed the many flies in the area on the dairy long after it closed. I was at my cousin's house in Wai'alae-Kahala just a couple of years ago and the flies are still thick. This is some 40-plus years after the dairy closed, so I think the flies just switched from cow pies to doggie-doo, and kept right on going.

Hind-Clark Dairy was mauka of Wai'alae in Niu Valley. They had a fine operation going on there, milk from Golden Guernsey cows, and a drive-in that sold great ice cream in those cookie-like waffle cones.

A big Foster & Klieser sign, that I'm sure was not sanctioned by the Honolulu Outdoor Circle, was next to the drive-in. The sign pictured a smiling, nice-looking cow with a caption above that read, "Our cows are never contented, they always strive to do better."

The Kamehameha Schools' farm was farther out, just before you reach Hawai'i Kai. They taught the boys how to raise pigs, chickens and dairy cows.

I guess you're tired of dairies by now, and I'd quit, except I must tell you there was no homogenizing when I was young. When it was first introduced it was said the homogenizing was not healthy for you.

The cream in the top half of Kaimi Dairies' bottled milk was so thick you could uncap the bottle, turn it upside down, and no milk would come out. You had to spoon out the thick cream first.

LAND SHELLS

Upon his death, C. Montigue Cooke gave his land-shell collection to the Bishop Museum in Honolulu. There are over 10,000 of these tiny treasures and they fill a number of wide, shallow drawers which can be found on the third floor of the annex building behind the museum.

Each tiny land shell variety is carefully catalogued and has a melodious name like Terra Crustacia Lavendria. They can be seen in a wide variety of colors and color combinations. Most shells are spiraled, about an eighth of an inch wide, and about half an inch long.

Although this hobby of C. Montigue's is a bit unusual, quite by accident I ran into a British gentleman in Singapore some years ago who also had a fine collection of several hundred species of land shells. He said he spent considerable time in research needed to identify the different species, and of course, he knew of C. Montigue Cooke's work in this area.

In a somewhat lighter vein, I must tell you that my primary interest in land shells results from my listening to the beautiful, high-pitched and crystal clear musical sound they produce. It is quite like the sound you can make by running your finger around the rim of a crystal glass of water.

Sometime, you might like to try lying quietly outside on the grass on a dark and very still night. If it is quiet enough, you could be lucky enough to hear the little critters serenading each other. Then, on hands and knees, you might softly creep up on them. When you are right above their soft singing, if you snap on a flashlight quickly, you might see your minute prey.

Perhaps you will find that listening to land shells, or hunting them at night, is best conducted when a very close friend accompanies you.

Hiking With My Father

My dad's only real sport was hiking. I went with him from the time he had to pack me on his back until I could manage for myself.

He was an amateur botanist, but his knowledge of Hawaiian flora was very professional. He knew both the Hawaiian and Latin names for most of our local plants. Father also knew about the uses of plants by the early Polynesian settlers, such as using the kukui nut as a candle or a cathartic.

He told me a romantic story that we still relate today, which is, if you pick an ohia flower it will rain.

Sometimes we hiked with others. I remember Albert Judd, a trustee of the Bishop Estate when my father was Chief Engineer, often went along with us.

Mr. Judd showed me how to make a leaf cup to use to drink water from a stream and how to get water from a travelers palm. As we went along he would grab small red Hawaiian peppers and pop them in his mouth. A real fire-eater!

Much later, when I was a partner with my father in the land appraisal business, I would do a lot of the hiking into places that were too rough for him and would describe the lay of the land. We would discuss the geology and best uses for the land, both current and future. We did appraisals at places such as Mōkapu, Waihino, Mākaha and Niu on O'ahu.

Hamburger Helpers

"Eh blah, luke da meats" meant "Hey brother, look at the good looking girls". There were other uses for the word "meat," of course, like "meet my meat" which translates into " shake hands with my girlfriend."

In the roaring '30's on O'ahu, the Mānoa Gang would come charging out of Mānoa Valley in Chris Farias' 4-door model T Ford with no top to cruise Waikīkī and check out the "meats." We would usually stop and give Sonny Sunstrom a hand in the building of his Kau Kau Korner.

Sonny's new drive-in was located at the intersection of Kalākaua Avenue and Kapi'olani Boulevard. We helped him with such jobs as spreading tar on the roof of the drive-in and gravel in the parking area. For the first day of the grand opening of K.K.K., we had carefully painted the words MEET THE MEATS AT KAU KAU KORNER in large letters on both sides of the Model T and stuck flowering branches from Poinciana trees on both sides of the windshield and at the rear end of the cab.

Our advertising effort netted us free hamburgers and milk shakes and kept Sonny Sundstrom's advertising budget low. Another benefit for us was the opportunity to "spark the meats" up close.

Tea Dancing at the Young Hotel

In the mid '30's, there was a roof garden on top of the Young Hotel Building (6th floor) where tea dances were held for young people. All the social climbers in town attended, and naturally I went along like a good boy.

At night a few years after tea dancing was pau (finished), the better bands from San Francisco, like Ted Weems, played there, usually for a month at a time. Giggi Royce's orchestra, though, was at the "Roof " for quite a number of years.

I was introduced to my first French 75 there. What a kick! They were made like a gin and tonic, but with champagne instead of tonic water. A true French 75, a la Paree during the First World War, was cognac in a champagne glass topped with champagne.

NAMES FROM THE PAST

We seemed to have more nicknames in the old days. Some of those I remember are: Butterball, Fella Boy, Old Lady Shingle, Dotsie Schenck, Airdale McPhearson, Wakie Mist, Conkie Borthwick, Fish Scales, Sqeeze Weller, Lamie Lucas, and Gomma Gomma Gomes. Then there was Bughouse Englehard, Punkie Nottage, Ewa Bird, Bumper Jiggles Jeffries and lots of Brothas, Sistas, Ahsuks, Titas, Keokis, Kimos, and Kawikas.

How come the younger squirts don't do that today?

KŪMŪ VS. TEETA

"Eh, spark da kūmū," was the label we gave any pretty and curvaceous girl when I was in my early teens and out with the guys.

Kūmū is the name of the goatfish, which in the early days, was kapu (off limits) to all but the ali'i (chief). It is also the Hawaiian word for good looking.

"Eh, luke da teeta," was the expression we used when we saw a former kūmū, now over the hill, crooked lipstick and a few misplaced curves.

We sometimes liked to say, "Eh teeta, show me your pearly toots." Many times this produced a smile revealing missing teeth.

"Teeta" might have been brought to us by the Spanish who arrived in Hawai'i in the pre-missionary days. It is short for Conchita and we used to say "teeta" which is localese for "tita."

Another word for a pretty girl that we generally used in the old days was "Tomato." We don't seem to hear this description in our language anymore, except during a domino or cribbage game amongst us septu- and octo-generians.

I wonder what the girls called *us* in those days?

TIN CAN ALLEY

During the summer of 1937, I worked as a laborer for Dillingham Construction. The job was building Doris Duke's mansion just on the Koko Head side of Diamond Head. I was assigned to the "cesspool gang." Besides me, there were two Hawaiians and a Portuguese guy.

We had to dig our way through compacted coral using pneumatic drills. The cesspool had to be dug to below ocean level, so we had to go down 60 feet. You looked up at the moon and the stars in the daytime when you were down that deep. My comment about it at the time was, "We have to dig this thing deep because of all the big shits that will be living here."

We worked until noon on Saturdays, which was payday. One Saturday I was invited to join the rest of the cesspool gang for beers in Tin Can Alley. Tin Can Alley was down in Iwilei just mauka of King Street along Nu'uanu Stream. There were several raunchy beer joints there, and I suspect a few houses of ill repute. I think the toothless ladies hanging around the bars were whorehouse retirees. All the customers were local, so after a couple of beers I took off.

As usual, the "cesspool gang" returned to work Monday morning and sweated out alcohol. Pee yoo!

BUICKS COST MORE THAN FORDS

When 'Iolani School was located up by Nu'uanu Cemetery, our headmaster, the very Reverend Stone, (Pōhaku was his Hawaiian name) sent a note home to our parents before Lent asking that they give money till it hurts, which they did.

But for old, snow-white-haired Rev. Stone, it was not enough, so a rather stern note about our failure to provide properly for our Lord was sent home and more money came forth.

A day or so after the Lenten season Rev. Stone drove onto campus in a brand-new Buick Roadmaster. We had a lot of fun pointing at our Lenten money driving by.

WHAT GOES AROUND, COMES AROUND

Fred Brown was my roommate during my last year in High School at Black Foxe Military Institute in California. Every now and then he invited me to spend the weekend with him at his home in San Diego. The thing I remember most about these weekends was seeing Dorothy Clark, Fred's beautiful girlfriend.

After graduation, Fred went home to San Diego and, in the fall, he entered Menlo College in Menlo Park, California to improve his grades so he could be accepted at Stanford.

Quite a number of students from Hawai'i also went to Menlo as a path into Stanford, including my friends Bob Williams and Eddie Lloyd. Eddie and I were cabin mates on the Lurline on our way back to school in September, 1941. I went to UCLA and Eddie went to Menlo College.

I lived in a fraternity house at UCLA along with one of our most brilliant students, Curly Evans, who was a physics major. Curly had a photographic memory and it was fascinating the way he could flip over page after page in a book every few seconds remembering everything on each page. Curly was very good looking and all the girls were after him. He could handle them all right, along with a large quantity of booze almost every night, plus still have time to attend classes and teach a physics quiz section for Professor Vern Knudsen, head of the physics department.

In November, 1941, Dr. Knudsen was appointed by our government to head the Naval Sound Laboratory in San Diego. The following June, when Curly graduated from UCLA, he was asked to accept a physicist's position at the Naval Laboratory by his old friend and professor, Dr. Knudsen. So, Curly headed off to San Diego to pursue his career.

Fred Brown kept plugging away at his studies at Menlo all through the summer so he could enter Stanford in the fall. Eddie Lloyd, however, decided to do something to free himself from the draft so he went to San Diego to work for Consolidated Aircraft.

Inasmuch as Eddie was going to San Diego, Fred asked him to say hello to his sweetheart, Dorothy. Eddie did more than this by marrying Dorothy.

About a year later, Eddie Lloyd left Consolidated and joined the U.S. Air Force becoming a pilot and flying a bomber over Germany. Curly Evans moved in with Dorothy.

At about the same time, Helen Duryea, a good friend and next door neighbor of mine in Mānoa, had married and moved to Tampa, Florida. Her husband, in the military service, was shipped overseas to do battle with the Hun.

The U.S. Navy then decided to move the Naval Sound Laboratories to Tampa, as testing new torpedoes and depth bombs was easier to do in the Gulf of Mexico than in the Pacific Ocean off San Diego.

Curly Evans, Dr. Knudsen and all the San Diego crowd

moved to Tampa where, curiously, Curly met Helen. Since housing was somewhat tight near the new Naval Labs, Curly moved in with Helen.

At a party of old friends in Southern California in 1946, Curly told me about his living arrangements with Dorothy and Helen. He was very complimentary, but at the same time, it is a small world, isn't it?

STEAMER DAYS

Steamer days were important in the Honolulu community before the war (WWII). Everyone arriving or departing had leis, some with so many they were up to their eyes and loaded on both arms. Arriving ships brought tears of happiness and the departing ones usually tears of sadness.

The SS Lurline and SS Matsonia were island favorites, with the Monterey and Mariposa and sometimes Dollar Lines ships like the President Cleveland were considered close seconds.

Fort Street near Aloha Tower, where the passenger ships docked, was a scene of great excitement. Hordes of people would be buying lei from the long line of lei sellers who were usually older Hawaiian ladies (some Chinese, though). Bargaining was normal, "One for fifty cents, three for a dollar."

On the departing ships, were parties, parties, and more parties, complete with kisses and many wet eyes as we bade loved ones and friends goodbye.

Pretty soon, "All ashore who's going ashore" was repeated several times over the loudspeaker system, followed by a long ear-shattering blast on the ship's whistle. Finally there was a last kiss and a hurried exit for almost all, with the exception of a few stragglers, who either jumped off the ship as it was slowly moving out of Honolulu Harbor or who paid for an unplanned trip to San Francisco.

Those of us who were seeing people off on the Matson Ships, pressed together on the open lānai deck of the second level at Aloha Tower. There we would wave aloha and try to catch hold of the end of the paper serpentines, or flower lei, thrown to us from departing friends on the ship.

The marvelous, and very loud, Royal Hawaiian Band was there in their starched, white, military style uniforms, blasting forth E Mea Ou Mea Ou Oi and Aloha Oe. Lena Machado, in her white uniform and perky white hat, sang along with the band with her beautiful and very strong soprano voice.

When the last line was cast off the dock, the ship would give three "Aloha" blasts on its whistle and would slowly head out of the harbor. When you left the dock and Aloha Tower, perhaps you would buy leftover lei from the lei ladies, formerly a dollar apiece, but now three for a quarter, for your new "honey" that night.

There are two things I almost forgot about the departing ship events: on the outboard side of the vessel: local boys were treading water and diving after coins thrown to them; the other event took place when the vessel was off Waikīkī nearing Diamond Head. There the ship's whistle would again sound three long "Aloha" blasts as a few teary--eyed passengers threw lei overboard to float away in the water. This meant "I'll come back." and many of them did.

On the ship, local girls would be busy sorting through their lei so they would have good ones to wear each night for dinner and dancing.* The best lei was always saved for the Captain's Dinner the last night out.

*The ship kept the lei under refrigeration, and if you smiled nicely and tipped your room steward well, he would deliver one of your almost-fresh, cool lei to you each night. In the evening, guests wore tuxedos and long formal gowns in first class.

STOWAWAYS IN THE EARLY DAYS

In the '20's and '30's, one of the most exciting events for passengers on the old Matson passenger ships took place at sea, when captured stowaways were transferred about three days out of either San Francisco or Honolulu. There always seemed to be stowaways.

Two ships, usually Matson owned, one headed to San Francisco, the other to Honolulu, would manage to navigate close to each other in mid-ocean and proceed to exchange stowaways. Excited passengers on deck would put down their sherbets or bouillon, or stop playing shuffleboard, in order to watch the transfer.

A lifeboat would be lowered and members of the crew would row the "culprit" across to the other vessel so that he could get a free ride in the other direction. Sometimes the sea was quite rough. When this happened, the spectators at the event were few!

After World War II ended, stowaways on Matson passenger lines sailing between the Mainland U.S. and Hawai'i became quite sophisticated and rarely were ever caught. They would simply walk aboard as though they were a member of the crew (of course many were friends of crew members) and sleep in someone's bed who was on watch or at work.

Food was easy to come by, and stowaways would even be handed out beer at the crew's "slop chest."

Upon arrival in port, the freeloader simply walked off the ship. "Aloha, and thank you for the nice trip."

AKUALELE - A GHOST THAT SALES THROUGH THE AIR (AKULELE MEANS METEOR. AKUA LAPU MEANS GHOST)

Once in a while, when traveling between Pu'uwa'awa'a and Waimea on a dark night, if you look carefully, you may see an akualele (ghost). I am told that akualele are really just moving balls of decaying vegetable matter that light up when blown across the range by the wind. Just try to explain that to a 10-year-old who is watching these ghostly balls of fire coming right at him!

AKUALELE AND DANDER ROSS

Alexander "Dander" Ross's mother, Bernice, was one of the Kupke girls. Another Kupke girl, Eda, was Martha "Tommy" Lowry's mother. For your information, Tommy married Jimmy Greenwell.

Auntie Bernice used to be my father's singing teacher. Dad used to run up and down the scale each morning with "Mommy may I moo," or something that sounded like that.

Dander married May Cunha, a local beauty, whose father wrote "Boola Boola," the Yale song. The above just to keep you in perspective.

Dander got a summer cowboy job in Kohala at the Kahuā Ranch and told me about how terrified he was one night by a Hawaiian ghost, an akualele.

He said he was on his way back to the ranch from Waimea, known then as "Kamuela" by most people, when out on the range an akualele appeared and sailed toward him. Dander said that it looked like a lighted long-sleeved shirt with the arms waving at him, trying to grab him.

"Fortunately," he said, "I reached the gate and closed it tight against that buggah, otherwise I make (die) for sure."

He said the ghost's arms even tried to grab him through the fence. One scary story, I think.

MILEAGE PLUS

Just about everything was 'monopolized' here in Hawai'i before World War II and for a few years afterwards. For example, many grocery stores gave their customers a choice between Del Monte canned tomatoes and any other Del Monte canned goods, and Best Foods was the only mayonnaise available.

It was difficult for large non-Big Five businesses to start up here in Hawai'i. Land was just not made available to people outside of the family. Finally, S. H. Kress was able to buy a piece of property from the Catholic Church, next door to the Cathedral on upper Fort Street on the fringe of downtown Honolulu. Years later Sears Roebuck was able to buy some acreage out of downtown Honolulu on Beretania Street across from the Mormon Church.

Pan American was the only airline serving Hawai'i, first with its flying boats, the Clippers, then later with DC-4s, and finally jets. Pan Am's monopoly remained firm with the backing of "Big Business" and the Honolulu Chamber of Commerce. Pan Am's board of directors was a cross-section of influential members in our business society.

Although sugar and pineapple were the territory's basic industries, tourism was to become our third biggest business, growing by leaps and bounds in the late '40's and '50's. As we all know, there is nothing bigger than the tourist industry here in Hawai'i today. A visitors bureau was started, and the members of the Hawai'i Visitors Bureau were volunteers, usually people associated with large private businesses. One year my father headed the bureau. This was during the time he was chairman of the board of trustees of the Bernice Pauahi Bishop Estate.

United Airlines had been trying to secure rights to fly into Hawai'i for some time, and began huge advertising and political campaigns. In this endeavor, it was publicized that Mr. Patterson, who was United's president at the time, had been raised in Wahiawā, O'ahu. This fact was aimed at the local people to make it look like he was "one of us."

Well, you might imagine the war that was waged between the two airlines and their supporters. While the federal government in Washington, D.C. had the final say on whether or not to break up the Pan Am monopoly, support from Hawai'i was important and the Hawai'i Visitors Bureau, with my dad as its president, capitulated in favor of United Airlines. Hearings were held in Washington and United was finally given permission to provide service to Hawai'i. I was working at a Big Five Company, Castle & Cooke, at the time and, with a touch of humor, my father asked me if I believed in monopolies.

Funny thing, the other day my wife Nancy found an old Pan Am handout packet containing soap, hand cream and perfume, which she gave away as a bridge prize. Unique antique.

LIQUOR RATIONING

During World War II, liquor was rationed in Hawai'i. Most of the time folks drank locally made "Five Islands" gin. It was horrible stuff; full of headaches.

One day, a couple of ladies I knew saw a long line of people, mostly service personnel. "Ah ha," they said, "some good booze must be for sale."

They stood in line for a while until a serviceman kindly mentioned that they were standing in a line of men waiting to visit a whorehouse.

Two more things to relate while on the subject: there were front and back entrances to many of the houses in the red-light part of town. The front was for service personnel, and the back entrance was for locals, mostly immigrant labor from the plantations.

Also, late in the war, General Richardson's wife thought it was absolutely dreadful for the U.S. Army to allow whorehouses. Since Hawai'i was under military rule at the time, the "houses of pleasure" were all closed down.

PIPI - MILK FOR OUR BABIES

In the late '40s and through the first half of the '50s, dairy cattle were shipped to Hawai'i from the Mainland U.S. in portable wooden cattle pens which were stowed on the open decks of ships. These milk cows were all very pregnant at the time they were put aboard, and stock tenders were sent along on the ships so they could help in the birthing of calves along the way.

The baby calves did not arrive in the islands, however, as the stock tenders heaved them overboard into the blue Pacific Ocean as soon as they were born. The reason for this calficide was that dairies bought milk cows and did not want to throw away good money raising baby calves.

Once again "economics" rears its ugly head.

PUA'A - LOCAL PORK IS ONO

Pork from pigs that were raised in Hawai'i and fed slops were always much preferred by our local population over mainland pork. So naturally, island pork sold in the market cost a lot more than the imported lean cuisine type of pork. My family, as did most, separated our garbage. Kitchen scraps were saved for the "pig man" in five-gallon used kerosene tins which he provided. The rest of our trash was picked up by the city's garbage trucks.

In the early years after World War II, large quantities of live pigs from the Mainland U.S. were shipped into Hawai'i. I thought this was the result of the tasty local pigs being over-consumed during the war years by G.I. Joes and others in our swollen population at that time. While this may have been part of the answer, I found out the malahini (mainland) porkers became kama'aina (local) as soon as they stepped ashore in Hawai'i Nei.

Their time as local residents was cut short, though, because they were immediately trucked from the ship to the local slaughterhouse. The next day "fresh island pork" was readily available in the market.

POLIO PLUS

In the late '40's, many neighborhoods in Honolulu contributed money to pay for the weekly service of mosquito trucks. Vehicles towing smoke-making machines on wheels made the rounds early in the evening, when the winds were light, spewing forth clouds of diesel smoke.

We could hear the truck coming and would beat a hasty retreat into our houses for a short while until the smoke dissipated.

The smoke was supposed to eradicate polio-carrying mosquitoes which thrived in the swamps and other moist places in our community. It did some good too. There seemed to be many less mosquitoes during this period.

Then it was discovered that the flies, not the mosquitoes, carried the polio virus, and so the night-fogging program came to a halt, and the mosquitoes flooded back into our neighborhoods again.

Just a little way down the street from our house in Lanikai, one person in each of three homes next door to each other was stricken with poliomyelitis. Those were very scary times.

FISHING IN KONA A FEW YEARS AGO

Although we went after marlin, we also fished for eating fish like mahimahi, ono and ulua. There were few charter boats then. Henry Chee, former president of Kona Rotary, had the best catch record. Other skippers used to mumble something about his going out with charters more than anyone else, so he was bound to catch more fish. Success breeds success.

From Kailua down to South Point, the ocean was dotted with solitary fishermen in their canoes. A dozen or so boats with radios talked back and forth about not much until someone got a big strike. Then it was fun to listen to all the commotion, even though it wasn't on your boat.

Sometimes when you passed Napo'opo'o, you would see Blue Frazier's (former manager of Dole on Lāna'i) sampan at anchor in the bay while he was talking over the radio from his lānai (porch) pretending he was fishing miles off Ho'okena.

At Miloli'i, the wives sat and gossiped in shallow water while they filled jars with 'opihi (limpet) pried off the rocks with table knives. Vana (sea urchins) were collected too, and the sharp, black spines were broken off by shaking them back and forth in a heavy wire mesh construction strainer. Broke da mouth!

Kona crabs, rich and delicious, were easy to get in those days. A friend of mine brought a box of frozen aku (tuna) heads for crab bait back to Kona from Tuna Packers in Honolulu. They were in the overhead rack on the Convair on the flight over and thawed a bit before landing in Kona. Pilau! (Stinky.)

We dropped about 10 crab nets with the aku heads attached off Kahalu'u Beach with long lines attached to coconut floats. We got about a hundred crabs in just two drops, letting someone off in between the first and second drops to get the pot boiling. Real ono (tasty) with beer.

I tired fishing already.

Huli Huli Goat (Turned on a Spit)

It was just about 50 years ago that I went to my first baby lū'au given by a Filipino family. The food was delicious, of course, with the exception of one dish I couldn't quite relish. That was the huli huli goat.

My friends had first force-fed vinegar into the goat to purify (and I guess flavor) its insides. Then after killing the animal in the orthodox way, they rammed a long steel rod through it from stem to stern, and rotated it over a wood fire. What really got me was the smell of the burning goat hair. Bon appetit.

Goat Riddance

At an earlier time in West Hawai'i, there were too many wild goats, so the ranches would have goat roundups. The goats would be herded by ranchers on horseback into valleys and then killed off in a great display of riding and riflery.

The dead goats did not go to waste, I am told, as they were flown to Honolulu and sold for $5.00 a head.

The Nottage Invitational

David Nottage is one of the best fishermen around. The annual Nottage Fishing Tournament was an event we always looked forward to with the fishing boats, carrying their lusty crews, leaving the Honolulu side of O'ahu for Kāne'ohe at daylight.

The boats fished all the way from Honolulu, around Koko Head, Rabbit Island, outside the Mokulua Islands and Mōkapu, finally making it into Kāne'ohe Bay and over to the Kokokahi side where the channel to the Nottage house and wharf was located.

There the boats (20 or 30 of them) tied up side by side. Fishermen would board each other's boats to enjoy lots of sashimi, beer, and gin & tonics. Then they would jump ashore to consume more beverages, pupus and grilled steaks. Crap games, cribbage and poker games went into full swing. No, there were no wahines invited until after the roughest part of the celebration was over, and then some of the wives showed up to drive their pooped out husbands home.

Once, after Dave had moved the Aukaka from Honolulu to Kāne'ohe, he tried to drum up some charter business with the U.S.

Marine Corps at the Kāne'ohe Marine Corps Air Station at Mōkapu by inviting the recreation officer from the base to attend the Nottage Tournament. A young U.S. Marine Corps major came aboard at Kewalo and we left port heading toward Diamond Head. When we were off Waikīkī, the major began to turn as green as a marine uniform and made several disparaging remarks about the spaghetti his wife cooked the night before. Just about opposite Diamond Head buoy, the major and his spaghetti parted company. We had only his fanny to look at from that point on as he hung over the stern all the way to Kāne'ohe.

I don't know whether or not David got any fishing boat charters from the Marines, or if the recreation officer interested his charges in things like hiking and archery rather than fishing.

An Overnight Trip to Moloka'i

Bill Fleming stayed up on deck looking up at the stars as the Aukaka sailed along toward the banks on the north side of Moloka'i. The boat was held steady to its course by its new Sperry gyrocompass. So confident was the skipper, David Nottage, that the boat would hold a true course all the way from Kewalo Basin to Moloka'i, that he, the crew, and guests all settled down for a nice four-hour nap, especially since no other craft were to be seen anywhere ahead on the ocean. Oh yes, it was safe all right.

It was a beautiful, cloudless night with, what seemed to Bill, to be millions of stars in the heavens. Once in a while a shooting star was seen squirting over to see a neighbor. He picked out the Big Dipper with its ladle and cup, but was surprised to see the ladle slowly moving around in a big circle. In fact, about an hour after leaving Kewalo, the ladle seemed to have moved around 180 degrees or so.

Since Fleming was a lawyer and not an astronomer, he was not sure if this moving around in a big circle by the Big Dipper was within the scope of astronomical fact. Then, as he was not sure, he raised himself to gunwale height and looked around. Everything over his right shoulder seemed fine, but by golly, when he peered towards the Aukaka's bow, there was the Royal Hawaiian Hotel about two hundred yards dead ahead with nice big waves breaking just 50 feet in front of the bow.

Needless to say, he aroused everyone pronto and now, wide-awake, David Nottage swung the wheel over hard right bringing the Aukaka once again in line with Moloka'i. Then David reset the gyro gear that had somehow snapped loose. Whew.

A Leisurely Voyage Around Moloka'i

A good place to start, if you are going crabbing, is Hawaiian Tuna Packers (Coral and Bumble Bee brands) in Honolulu where you could get free aku (tuna) heads.

Aku heads are tied firmly to the center of the crab nets which are lowered into deep water. The north side of Moloka'i was a dandy place to drop the nets. A long line from the nets is tied to a coconut or a plastic Clorox bottle which floats and tells you where the crab net is located.

It was about 40 years ago when I made my last Aukaka trip with Dave Nottage to Moloka'i, but if my memory serves me properly, we put out about 12 crab nets and at the same time put on a large pot of water to boil. When the last crab net was tossed over the side with its coconut float, we went around and hauled up the first one we had tossed over, then the second one and so forth.

Each net came up full of crabs hanging on for dear life because they did not want to lose their share of the tasty fish head. "Dear life" did not last too long, because as soon as they were plucked off the nets, they were plopped into the steaming pot. What a glorious feast we all had on the rich and sweet crab.

Going down the east coast of Moloka'i, past beaches and verdant tall cliffs with tumbling waterfalls, is much more interesting and beautiful than the other side of the island where the town of Kaunakakai is located. We sailed past beautiful beaches and the settlement for Hanson's Disease at Kalaupapa.

We pulled in close to shore and anchored for the night opposite a beautiful waterfall that cascaded straight down from about one thousand feet above. At the base of the falls, a freshwater pond had been carved out of the rock by the water action which was forever pounding down from above. This trip took place many years before we became gripped by ecology, so no one complained when we poured a whole carton of Rinso Laundry Soap into the base of the falls. The result of our action was a gigantic bubble bath and we all had a hilarious "in the buff" swim. Wow, Wee, Wow!

The next day we sailed around the south end of Moloka'i with the Island of Maui rising next door, and down the western shore past Paul Fagin's ranch with his cream colored Charlet cattle. The seas were very calm, and as we came in toward land I spotted a very large glass ball float which had broken loose from a Japanese fishing net. I still have that big glass ball here in Kona.

Shortly after that, we saw people on the beach trying to corral a full-grown axis deer. The deer was so desperate to get away he plunged into the ocean in an attempt to flee his pursuers. The ladies on the Aukaka decided they had to save the animal from drowning, so a small punt was put over the side with four rescuers aboard. I wondered where they would put the deer if they did rescue it. As the punt slowly motored toward the deer, from the Aukaka I noticed that the people on the beach were becoming quite agitated. In fact, they begin firing rifles at the punt and the "mother" ship. Little splashes could be seen near the punt and more started appearing near the Aukaka. Fortunately, we were floating out of range and were definitely too far away by the time the little deer was saved by putting a rope around its neck and dragging it alongside the punt until it could be hoisted aboard the Aukaka.

After letting the animal go back into the wild on a deserted beach a few miles down the coast, it occurred to us that the people shooting at us were upset because we had stolen their dinner.

David Nottage's mother had a vacation cottage ashore on Moloka'i, so we stayed there a couple of nights before sailing back to Kāne'ohe on O'ahu.

A Cribbage Lesson

Just about once a month, four to six of us Kona cribbage "greats" would assemble at the Aukaka for a day of fishing and cribbage. Of course, I was there as the last inter-island singles champion of a tournament that got its start in the late forties. Ahem!

For our cribbage games aboard the Aukaka, Fred Schatthauer, Dick Frazier, Jim McQuaid, Dr. Keith Nesting, the skipper Dave Nottage, and myself made up the usual gang.

Early in the morning the first thing put aboard, after fuel of course, was plenty of ice. This was necessary to cool down any fish caught as well as to keep the refreshments for the cribbage players cooled down. We shared the cost of pupus, bloody mary mix, beer and vodka. Sometimes though, Chartie Nottage, David's better half, would cook us up a big batch of rice and kanaka stew which was a real treat. Dick Frazier usually did the pupu buying at KTA supermarket, as the people there treated him with great reverence and respect for some reason or other.

We would pile aboard the boat at Honokōhau with all of our provisions, and cast off trying to drape the two stern lines onto the dock rather than into the water. As we eased away from the dock, David, the most nimble of us, undid the bow line from its buoy and draped it over the top of the buoy for an easy grab with a boat hook when we returned home. After we cleared the green buoy at the entrance to the port, we would throw the steering onto the "iron mike" with the gyro compass set more-or-less toward South Point.

Way back on one of our earlier trips, sometimes only four of us went out and cruised to South Point playing cribbage all the way. When we were tied up hours later at Honokōhau, the skipper of the charter boat in the slot next to the Aukaka said, "David, we saw you practically all day, but did not see anyone steering the Aukaka. We tried to raise you on the radio, but I guess you didn't have your radio on." David replied, "Of course you didn't see anyone, we were playing cribbage." The charter skipper could not think of a way to reply to this and the matter was dropped. We decided then that we had better take at least five people along on future "fishing" trips in order to have a lookout.

We would always put lines out in case a fish decided to get caught. We believed our wives thought we were more interested in going fishing then playing cribbage. Ha. Anyway, the lures bounced along on fairly short lines, more on top of the waves than below, but you know something, a fish always interrupted our cribbage game. Still, it was good to take home a large hunk of fresh mahimahi, spearfish or ahi.

On our last cribbage voyage on the Aukaka, we headed straight out past the green buoy at the entrance of Honokōhau for about seven miles. Then, with no other boats in sight we came to the left about 90 degrees, slapped in the iron mike, and headed straight for South Point. There were only four of us that day and we wanted to use our full powers of concentration on the game. So for about six hours we headed south with the game only briefly interrupted by time-outs to mix bloody marys or get a beer.

Finally the "Commander" of our ship took a sighting of the land and said, "My god, I thought we were off of Miloli'i, but that's South Point." One of our crowd said, "Oh Oh, I told the ole' lady I'd be home by five because we have company coming to the house."

Captain Nottage said it looked like we could make it back by 6:30pm as we turned back toward Kailua and picked up the speed a knot or two.

Back we went toward port, playing our favorite game, with the fish lures bouncing along on top of the waves. Near home, just off Ka'iwi point, we had a double strike and wasted no time in reeling in two large mahimahi's.

Nobody was scolded for being late as everybody arrived home with a meal in hand.

LAST TIME AT BAT

As May turned to September and finally hit December, it became harder and harder for us older guys to get in and out of the Aukaka. We seriously considered hiring a small crane or "cherry picker" to lower us in and pull us out of the boat. Things got so bad that when David was going back aboard one day, he slipped off the dock and fell down onto the stern of the boat slamming himself into the fighting chair. He broke his clavicle, four ribs, an arm and his glasses.

The last time we went out as a group, cribbage was hot and heavy as usual and right in the middle of the game, zing went one of the reels. Since David had a good hand, he said, "Wait until we finish this hand. Maybe the S.O.B. will shake himself off."

But he didn't, and Schatthauer hauled in a 175-pound Marlin without much fuss.

THE LAWS OF THE SEA

The Aukaka was leaving Miloli'i, after some fun in the sun and a visit with Bill Hodgins, just about sashimi and cocktail time. Nottage pointed the boat out to sea, then both he and his lively crew set to carefully slicing an aku for sashimi and mixing some shoyu and mustard for sauce.

There is a long shallow reef which stretches out under water quite a ways at Miloli'i, and somehow the boat got turned a little, running right into it, ripping large holes in the boat below the waterline. All hands abandoned ship and made their way to safety leaving the poor Aukaka all alone, struggling to stay afloat and subject to scavenging by the people in the neighborhood.

The last beach house on the North side of the bay was Buggie Carlsmiths'. He was not only one of Hawai'i's greatest golfers at one time, but in his mumu, he became a silent watcher of the tragedy that befell the Aukaka. Captain Nottage yelled over to his friend Buggie that he would be back during the week to remove what he could from the boat. Upon his return, he visited the wreck and found that little of value remained.

According to Dave Nottage, Buggie had salvaged a number of items of value from the boat but, since the Aukaka had been abandoned, under the law it became open season for scavengers.

TIGER VS. HAMMERHEAD

Kāne'ohe Bay on O'ahu is home to two major families of sharks. North, towards Punalu'u, on the other side of Coconut Island, is the ancestral home of the tiger shark. South, on the other side of the island where the Kāne'ohe Yacht Club is located, hammerhead sharks have grandfather rights.

This is nice since with this "agreement," the fiercer tiger sharks do not "hop the fence," so to speak, to eat water skiers on the yacht-club side. Also, the hammerheads have a comparatively smaller mouth (I think) and skiers and swimmers are pretty safe on the yacht-club side of the bay

I believe, too, that hammerhead sharks are born with nicer dispositions than tiger sharks. This attitude may be enhanced by the good behavioral training that many of them receive at the University of Hawai'i's shark study program on Coconut Island in Kāne'ohe Bay before they are released into the wild.

Go Rainbows! Go Warriors!

THE CLOVEN HOOF SANCTION

Jimmy and Betty Wilder's home was out at Koko Head on Portlock Road. This was before the "city" of Hawai'i Kai was built, and the area was considered "country." There was a dairy and Earl Thacker's dude ranch across the highway at that time.

Very early one morning, Jimmy heard something making a racket on his lānai. When he went out to investigate he found a cow there. Jimmy was not sure whether to call the police or the humane society, so he called his lawyer, Tommy Waddoups, on the telephone.

"What'll I do?" Jimmy asked Tommy, after he described the situation.

Tommy, not happy at being awakened so early in the morning, replied "Shoot the son of a bitch," and hung up the phone.

So the cow died at the hands of Jimmy Wilder, and to this day I haven't heard how things were settled with the owner of the cow.

KANAKA BREAKFAST

Our loyal employees came to work nice and early, particularly the outside men (the claims inspectors). Their work was lined up for the day well before 8am, and then they were out of the office like a shot.

Alan Sonoda, Bill Borges and Arthur Kim were among the early birds, and they drove their unmarked company cars out of the parking lot without wasting any time, headed for their first customer of the day.

This was not always the case, however.

There were a few small cafes tucked away in Kaka'ako, Kalihi, Kaimuki and elsewhere at the time which catered to the 'ōpū (stomachs) of Hawai'i's multinational working force. Our noble inspectors headed to one of these joints where they ordered their favorite breakfasts.

They would order two or three eggs up or over, that were served on top of a mountain of rice. Side orders of hash-browned or french-fried potatoes, along with Portuguese sausage or corned-beef hash or bacon, would arrive heaped on the same large plate. The waitress's thumb was usually found under there somewhere, to be licked by her immediately after delivery to her customer.

Condiments were the usual Tabasco sauce, shoyu, and catsup. One, two or all of these were used, although Koreans, like Arthur Kim, tended to go a little heavy on the Tabasco.

Nowadays, I believe they call this kind of breakfast "Loco Moco."

JIM LUKE'S HOTEL (HĀWĪ)

Business got better for Luke's Hotel in Hāwī, North Kohala, when Hawaiian Airlines stopped flying into the Upolu Airport. This was because driving over to Kohala from the Kamuela (Waimea) Airport and back consumed so much driving time, you had to stay in Kohala overnight. So Jim Luke added a new wing onto his hotel.

Checking into the hotel was interesting. A first-time visitor would wander into what seemed to be the logical entrance to the lobby. This was the restaurant, and he would be told to check into the hotel "next door." Next door did not mean the house next door, it meant the room next to the restaurant.

The check-in parlor, which was right next to the dining area, could have been reached quite easily by walking right through to the other end of the restaurant. But no one told you this, so you would pick up your suitcase, back out of the restaurant, and then walk along outside until you found a door at the far end of the building.

In you went, to find what appeared to have been a former soda fountain. There was a low counter with swivel chairs in front of it, with shelves behind containing the necessities of hotel life such as toothpaste and cigarettes. No one would be there, of course, so you would stick your head around the corner into the restaurant and someone would say, "Een da keechin."

The kitchen was reached from either the back of the restaurant or the hotel lobby. There you would find Jim Luke, hat on, sitting in a chair reading the Honolulu Advertiser. Back to the 'lobby" you went with Jim, signed the guest register, and were handed the skeleton key to your room in the new wing, along with directions on how to get there.

After walking around the back of the restaurant and kitchen, you came to what Jim referred to as the "garage." It was big enough for about six cars but was being used as the laundry, a tack room, and a dog kennel.

Rarely was the entrance to the new wing visible because it was behind several rows of bed sheets hanging up to dry. After stepping around a few sleeping dogs, sawhorses with saddles resting on them, and ducking under a few sheets, you were able to find the new wing.

The rooms were plain four-wall jobs with bathrooms located between two rooms for the comfort of the occupants of each room. The walls were paper-thin, tongue-in-groove and, of course, no radio or TV. Not exactly a place for honeymooners.

One time when I was a guest at the Luke Hotel, Jim asked me and a friend to have dinner with him. He said he was going to barbecue a thick steak for us from a cow he had killed just that morning. About five o'clock that afternoon, we saw Jim fanning some kiawe charcoal in a portable barbecue he had set up just outside the garage-laundry-tack room-dog kennel entrance to the hotel. Sparks and smoke were flying everywhere. but mostly into the garage.

We had dinner about seven o'clock. The steak was about four

inches thick and the inner three inches were blood rare. The steak knives were very sharp, but our 40-year-old teeth were not sharp enough to chew "Old Bessie."

KOHALA'S ANNUAL SHARK HUNT

A grand event that took place in Kohala was the annual shark hunt. There were many spectators there to witness the "fun," including the Honolulu jet-set who flew in to the Upolu Point landing strip.

First, a sick or makule (old) ditch-trail mule was killed and made bloody to attract the sharks. The animal was bound up and then, after being tied to a long, stout rope to keep it from drifting to sea, was thrown into the ocean.

When the sharks came swimming to this lū'au, the hunters shot at them. The sharks, becoming wounded and bloody, attacked and chewed up each other.

Once when the rope keeping the mule close to shore became untied, a very brave (?) Filipino from the Kohala plantation jumped into the water and retied the line to the mule.

I remember the last hunt was disappointing, as the sharks, while invited, did not attend.

FLY CASTING FOR TROUT IN HAWAI'I

Did you know there are trout swimming around in a couple of places at the northern end of the Big Island of Hawai'i? I'm not going to tell you where to find these spots, but there were fly-casting clubs in both Honoka'a and Hāwī. Members fished for trout in our colder mountain waters.

The cold water in the mountain streams kept the trout flesh nice and firm, and the generous supply of bugs we have here in Hawai'i kept the trout big, fat, and juicy. Real ono (tasty)!

FAVORITE RESTAURANTS - O'AHU

Aside from Chinese restaurants and saimin joints, my favorite restaurants were, The Wagon Wheel, when Sam Nussbaum had it, along with The Tropics, Trader Vic's, Canlis Broiler, and Don The Beachcomber's.

Sam Nussbaum was one of many, many owners of The Wagon Wheel. Around 1935, the family went there for his famous mustard steak. This was a great thick sirloin. Sam himself would mix butter with Coleman's dry mustard right at the table, then slice the steak in strips, which he dunked in the mustard, butter, and steak juices before serving it.

Two of the things I remember about Sam were the Shriner's button he wore, and his big, loose, lower lip. I was always afraid he would slurp saliva onto the steak.

The Tropics in Waikīkī was owned and operated by Tony Guerrero. He put out an excellent salad with his own Tropics' dressing along with some very tasty thick teriyaki steaks. Tony was married to Peaches, who had been the little, black-haired girl in 'Our Gang" comedies a long time ago. They lived in Wai'alae Kahala next to Alec Castro's. My cousin Anita Rodiek lived on the other side of the Castros.

Trader Vic's was across the street from what is now the Blaisdell Center on Ward Street at King. Victor Bergeron opened it with a partner, Granville Abbott, a rich guy from Oakland, California.

Trader Vic's had good pupus and excellent Mandarin Chinese food. But the piece de resistance for me, anyway, was their New York Steak with a tasty Chinese spiced glaze on it. Another attraction at Trader Vic's was the tropical decor, with large glass floats from Japanese fish nets, blow fish, and oodles of maritime objects like ships' binnacles, old hawsers, and red and green ships' running lights.

The tropical drinks were interesting. My favorite was called a "Tonga," but on dates I used to order "Scorpions," a rum drink which came in a big bowl with two straws and a gardenia floating on top. It was supposed to loosen up your date, if you know what I mean! It never worked in my case, though.

I first went to Canlis Broiler when it was down on Kalākaua, Diamond Head of the Moana Hotel. It was a little hole in the wall, but the food, particularly the steaks, was very good. Pete Canlis was the headwaiter. Canlis operated a catering service as well as the small restaurant. Later Canlis opened up in a very fancy place across from the Kūhiō Theater in Waikīkī. It became a favorite place for many of us. One outstanding feature at Canlis was the full-sized, upside-down, decorated Christmas tree which hung from the ceiling in the bar area at Christmas time each year.

Don the Beachcomber, who had changed his name to Don Beach during World War II, was on the mauka side of Kalākaua

Avenue across from where the old Outrigger Canoe Club used to be. It featured a nice tropical setting with large, gently waving fans. If you were seated along the back of the restaurant, you sat on high-backed, wicker, "peacock" chairs. The food, Chinese and American, was okay but the Hawaiian music that went with it was excellent. Sam Kapu and Rosalie Stevens used to put out a great Ke Kali Nei Au (the Hawaiian wedding song).

The place had been built without much money changing hands. Fortunately for us, we had a friend named Fitzsimmons who was a contractor. Don owed him about $3,000, so he had to take his money out in trade. We were guests there on many occasions.

Carla Beach, Don's wife (I think she was from Honduras), played tennis at the Diamond Head courts. Once, we went to a cocktail party at their rather small house in Kahala across the street from Black Point Road (of Mamie Stover World War II fame). Carla had many male friends and kept her own apartment somewhere in Waikīkī. She knew the first astronauts, who came to Hawai'i to practice their moonwalk on the rough, barren lava found in Pōhakuloa on the Big Island. Carla claimed she had played mixed doubles with Stan Smith at Wimbledon. Interesting girl.

Other restaurants among my favorites were the Chinese places in downtown Honolulu. Wo Fat's was always good. Many of these restaurants were very small, and the help spoke only Chinese. Some only served dim sum, and others were one price, eat--as-much-as-you-can places. Hot dishes would come pouring out of the kitchens to be placed on lazy susans in the middle of round tables.

Frequently, the only other haole (white) I would see in that part of Chinatown was Frank Judd. He knew a good thing.

THE REPRESENTATIVES CLUB

The "Rep" Club began its life in Honolulu some years prior to World War II as a sportsman's club. A group of young businessmen banded together to sponsor an annual track and field event for the local high schools. It was named the "Representative Relays" and was a big event for both the schools and the general public. I was not really a track man but I always looked forward to going to the relays.

After the war, when I became bombed out on the Junior Chamber of Commerce, someone asked me to join the Representatives Club, which I did. By then the public school system had decided they did not need private sponsorship of a public and private school sports activity, and so we were excused.

But despite losing their primary program, the club went on meeting at the Commercial Club every Thursday noon, with good speakers on current events. We were much like a medium-sized Rotary or Kiwanis club. There were about 75 active members from the business and sports community. I was President in 1954. We never got back into sponsoring sports events. Instead, we became known for our famous (or infamous) annual stag party.

This stag event kept the membership intact for years. These parties were like a three-ring circus, with live strip-teasers on stage, porno movies in another area, and a crap game which lasted all night.

We had to watch out for police raids at these events, and usually donated to the Vice Squad's favorite charity by way of protection. Someone (or could it have been someone's wife?) ratted on us every year, but only once did we actually get raided.

That was the year our party was held at Wai'alae Country Club. When the cops poured in, we poured out. Luckily, there were several doors and windows in our party room.

Ward Russell, with the telephone company and a budding candidate for the Territorial House of Representatives, dove out a window and escaped into the tall sorghum growing next door at Locey's Wai'alae Dairy. The police were kind to us, though, and nothing happened.

Some of the members I can recall offhand were: Dougie Guy, Jimmy Greig, Thurston Twigg-Smith, Tommy Kalukukini, Johnny Bustard, Dave Pietsch, Pat Black, Dr. Bob Millard, Bill Kea, Carl and Buddy Farden, Tom Prentice, Bob Midkiff, Bob White, Benny Marks, Bill Fleming, Buddy Davis, Jim Lovell. And there were many, many more.

THE PACIFIC CLUB

Founded in 1851, the Pacific Club in Honolulu first went under the name of "The Mess," and then "The British Club," before succumbing to its present name. In 1930, for survival, the club merged with the University Club in Honolulu and thus, this fine-old club lives on unto this day.

My Granduncle, Paul Neumann, who was attorney general for both King Kalākaua and Queen Lili'okolani, was a member. My Uncle George Rodiek was also a member, but was "excused" because of unfounded aggressive German war activity during World War I.

When I was very young my father was a member of the University Club which was located in a large old mansion on Richards and Alakea Streets. I visited the club with my father, but due to my early age, all I remember about the place was the long stairway with many steps climbing up to its entrance, and then a long "L" shaped lānai (porch) which wrapped around the club to the left of the front doors.

There were numerous billiard tables on the lānai with pool tables inside the clubhouse next to the dining room. I remember hearing the constant click of score tabs as they were flicked along wires adjacent to each pool or billiard table. This was the extent of my memory of the University Club.

In the early days, the Pacific Club was like the University Club in that the lānai, and much of the inside dining room area, was given over to billiards and pool tables. There was a small library, where on Sundays families could come to dinner with a male member of the club. I remember we all spoke in whispers. Women and children were otherwise not allowed to enter this exclusive all-male club.

For sports in those days, besides pool and billiards, there was a swimming pool, a card room, and a very fine bar. Cottages on the premises were available for rent to male members who were bachelors, or for husbands who were temporarily or permanently separated from their wives.

When I joined the club in 1948, Bill Wise, Jack Eagle and Ward Russell were among those who occupied the cottages. Occasionally, cottage inhabitants and their buddies enjoyed some fine sport.

The Pacific Club was a downtown club for men until early in the '60's when women became privileged to use a portion of the facility and where a ladies card room could then be found. At that time, paddle tennis was enjoyed by all sexes.

Annual paddle tennis and volleyball matches were, and still are being held, and in the "old days," the best athlete we had was Jack Eagle. He played two-man and four-man volleyball matches, and then swung into men's singles, doubles, and mixed doubles paddle tennis matches.

I recall one year when he won all of the matches and preceded each event by swallowing a stand-up martini, olive and all. Maybe Jack had something to prove because with a name like "Eagle," his ancestry must have included some American Indian. Who said

Indians can't drink?

Later the Pacific Club members built a beautiful new clubhouse with many new facilities. In addition to a new dining room, the last male sanctuary, the Card Room, was given a face lift. At the back of its beautiful bar is a lovely Hitchcock mural of Kaua'i's Waimea Canyon. Bartenders Taki and Earnest made sure members had their special daiquiris or martinis. In the late afternoons or early evenings when a phone call came in for an overdue husband, these skilled purveyors of booze would hold a hand over the receiver and diplomatically ask, "Mr. Jones, are you here?"

The card room was a haven for the world's best cribbage players and I was there a lot. There were some pretty terrible bridge players and some fine domino players to be found in the card room. In the normal 11am to 2pm luncheon crowd, there would be the regular Castle & Cooke, Davies and Amfac cribbage tables, along with mixtures of businessmen at other tables from all walks of life in Honolulu plus a sprinkling of visiting members from the neighbor islands and many retirees.

A few years after moving back to the Big Island of Hawai'i in 1984 to live, I was a dues paying, neighbor-island member. I rarely went to the club when I visited Honolulu, so I finally resigned from the Pacific Club after figuring out that while it might look good in the obituary column to say that I had been a member, it served no other purpose that I could see.

Some say it was the original home of the two-martini lunch.

LOVE'S LABORS NOT LOST

When Persis Bacon Middleton first came to live with her children in Lanikai, Bill Middleton was there. We were not too sure whether Bill had replaced Curtis Bacon or not, and Persis left us guessing.

A number of us were invited to Persis's house for Thanksgiving dinner while Curtis Bacon was in town visiting his family. With both men at her house, we decided that whichever man carved the turkey could be classified as the "husband." Persis got around that by ordering Tom Prentice to do the carving. At a later time we learned that Bill Middleton was the head "turkey."

As the years went by, Bill had a problem. It was mental, but alcohol seemed to cause a lot of it, causing a lot of problems for Persis and her family. He got worse and worse, but I didn't bring you here for a treatise on mental deterioration - or did I?

One weekend the Prentices, and the Persis Bacon Middleton families, were at Kawela Bay near Kahuku on O'ahu. Bill was trying to sleep it off in the water, lying on his back on a surfboard. The surfboard started drifting out of the bay, into the deep water, on its way to Japan. The kids saw this and reported it to Fuzzy Prentice. Fuzzy found Persis and said, "Bill's asleep on a surfboard that's floating out to sea. Should we rescue him or just let him float away?" "Oh, no!" replied Persis. Bill was saved and rose to see another day.

Dr. Quisenbury

In the mid-'60's, I sometimes played tennis with a Dr. Quisenbury, chief pathologist for the State of Hawai'i, at the Punahou School tennis courts.

At about that time, mysterious deaths of young, single Filipinos were being reported in the Honolulu press. I think there were some 12 men in their 20's and early 30's who died of heart failure in less than a year, usually in the middle of the night.

During a breather at the courts one day, Dr. Quisenbury mentioned that after months and months of trying to learn the cause of these "mystery" deaths, it was determined that these young Filipino males had died from eating African snails. The poisons had accumulated in the snails from the poisonous plants they ate. This is what did in these young men.

But, you might ask, why only single young Filipino males?

Right after World War II, the sugar and pineapple industries in Hawai'i needed new blood to work on the plantations. Single male laborers from the Philippines were brought to Hawai'i to work in the fields. Snails were obviously a normal food in the diet of these young men from the Philippines. The snails they ate back home were either purged by mothers or wives of poisons, or the snails did not feed on poisonous plants. No one purged the Hawaiian snails.

Les Gourmet de Pūpū Society, Inc.

About 50 years ago, on Steve Wilcox's birthday, Allen invited a group of friends to meet at Trader Vic's for dinner. They enjoyed drinks and good pūpū (hors d'oeuvres) while they waited for all of the guests to arrive.

By the time all were assembled, they had consumed so many

pūpūs, they decided not to eat dinner. They decided then they would meet once a month, at each of their houses in turn, for a pūpū party.

Thus, the club was started. Betty Hodgins, who understood the French language, coined the name "Les Gourmets de Pupu Society, Inc." From then on the group met each month with the pūpū getting fancier and fancier.

The Pūpū Club, or as it's known by its formal name, Les Gourmets De Pūpū Society, Inc., is still going strong. Well, here in Kona at least. Most of the members, however, are 50 years older than when the group was formed. We now go home from our B.Y.O.B. pūpū parties by 8pm.

There was a time in Honolulu when home-made music and crap games went on until well after midnight. Now, not only do we get sleepy early, but our fingers aren't nimble enough for 'ukuleles or guitars, and our voices quiver a bit.

We used to go hog wild with our pūpū recipes and still do to a certain extent, although Costco is our big helper now. Imagination, with assistance from cookbooks, also helped. I especially remember a pūpū that was brought by a lady member. She had carefully collected African snails, and proceeded to feed them lettuce leaves for two weeks, in order to purge them of any accumulated poisons from oleander leaves, or other such poisonous plant life that they ate.

After the purge, she dumped the little beasts (or bugs, should we say) into a frying pan with lots of butter and garlic. Finally, she put each one into a regular, store-bought, French escargot shell and brought them to the pupa party.

Since we were all brave souls, and used to the unusual, no one regurgitated after they were told that the snails were "African," our number one garden enemy.

P.S.: As members of Les Gourmets de Pūpū, we all know how to use escargot forks.

Hawaiian songs were generally sung at these parties, along with Bobby Evans, playing the guitar, Frank Judd on bass fiddle, and Cass Fitzsimmons (now Richards), Dave Pietsch and others playing the uke ('ukulele). Being island bred and born, most of the wahines could do a mean hula. Other entertainment included shooting craps, usually taking place in a bedroom.

The pūpū party generally lasted well past midnight, because in those days, who went home from a party before then?

I joined several years after the group got going and my first meeting was at a dinner dance at the Royal Hawaiian Hotel. I asked Allen Wilcox who the president was, and he answered, "You." So you can see it was a pretty loose, happy little group.

Many years later, when we returned to Kona from Southeast Asia, Saudi Arabia and other places, we found many of the Honolulu members had retired and moved to Kona. Happy days! We were once again included in the Kona Branch of Les Gourmets de Pūpū. Somewhat older, of course, and without the voices, instruments, or pizzazz to play music, sing, shoot craps, and stay up late.

A few years ago at one of our annual meetings, I suggested we bring in some young blood, but looking around the room at members, all I could see were icy stares. Oh well, time marches on. But I do dread the thought of having a pūpū party some day at some retirement facility.

THE PILL

Nicky Rutgers' mother was a Johnson of the Johnson & Johnson baby powder family, but outside of a little more than the normal use of Band-Aids, we rarely heard Nick discuss his maternal connection.

About 50 years ago, we often shared rides driving back and forth to work from Kailua to Honolulu over the old curvaceous Pali Road. Traffic was usually very heavy on both sides of the business day, and to help pass the time on the long, slow ride home, we would have long discussions on just about anything, including any jokes we may have heard that day.

I recall sharing a story with Nicky as we rode home one day about methods for birth control. This was before the "pill." I asked him if he had heard about the two new wonder drugs for birth control and he answered, "No, what are they?" I replied that one was "sulfa denial" and the other was "no assatal."

Loyal to the core, Nick answered, "Yes, I believe Johnson & Johnson are already putting them out."

ILLEGAL STUFF

An entrepreneur we knew made a good income for himself by stealing Parker Ranch cattle. He never seemed to get caught, and a story went around that he was so well liked by the Parker Ranch people, they looked the other way and did not interfere with this man's nefarious business.

Most of his pilfered beef was sold to small butcher shops in Ahualoa and Honoka'a, which he delivered to his buyers late at night in an old battered pickup truck.

He was finally caught one night with a truckload of branded Parker Ranch beef because he had used a truck with license plates that were four years old. In those days, our license plates had different colors each year.

THE PIPES, THE PIPES ARE CALLING

Shortly after World War II, the new personnel in the plumbing department at the Dole Iwilei plant needed to replace the old underground water pipes. They looked high and low for the original plans of the plumbing layout, but they were not to be found.

It turned out that someone knew of a very famous "water witcher" in Vermont, so the company hauled him over to Honolulu to locate the pipes. He was very successful in doing this and saved Dole a lot of money.

This same Vermont gentleman was hired by the Bishop Estate to find fresh water in Kona. I am told that 167 wells were drilled, and while the expert did find some fresh water, most of the wells produced brackish water.

JOE LUKELA PULLS THE PLUG

Long before Henry J. Kaiser developed Hawai'i Kai on O'ahu, the Bernice Pauahi Bishop Estate fish ponds on Maunalua Bay were leased to one Joe Lukela. He trapped fingerlings from the ocean through pond gates which opened from Maunalua Bay. When the fish grew to man-size, Joe took them to the fish markets on King Street in downtown Honolulu.

Well, progress reared its ugly head and homes were built all along the beach at Portlock Road. These homes festered with children who loved to water ski, and boat fishermen who loved to fish. At least half of the bigger boats parked in Maunalua Bay weren't even owned by Portlock residents.

Joe Lukela witnessed all of this growth and the great churning of water by the boats and people in his bay. He complained to the Bishop Estate trustees that all of these boats were scaring away his fish. His harvest of mullet was growing smaller and smaller.

The trustees, in their wisdom and much like our government, did nothing about their tenant's problem. Joe became angrier and angrier with both the Bishop Estate, and the happy, laughing, pleasure-boat people who had intruded into his bay.

So one dark, moonless night, it is said, Joe Lukela and some friends rowed cautiously out into the bay and quietly drilled holes below the waterline of every boat they could find.

I want to tell you the next morning, before people in the beachfront homes even had breakfast, they looked out in astonishment at the bay and saw that their whole fleet of boats had been sunk! Phones rang and people gabbed, and all of them were mighty huhū (angry). They, of course, thought they knew who had performed this nefarious act and pointed their quivering fingers at Joe Lukela.

The police came, the Bishop Estate trustees came, and even some very sharp lawyer types came, but none of them could ever pin the rap on Joe Lukela.

DAN – A HAPLESS ROMANTIC

Dan didn't know what to do. In a way, you might say he screwed up and I became involved in trying to solve the mess because he was a damn fine employee, and I didn't want to lose him. It all happened this way:

Dan was an attractive Japanese, and I knew he had eyes for a saucy little Korean lass. He was our best insurance adjuster and she was a clerk typist in the office. After watching them for a while, I decided I had better call Dan in for my usual "Don't dip your pen in the company ink" advice.

Although I didn't know it at the time, the ink was already on the floor, and Dan suddenly went AWOL. Although we looked everywhere, we couldn't find him. Then his Korean girlfriend came into my office and, after considerable sobbing, said that she was pregnant and would I please find Dan.

I was frankly very worried about Dan, to the extent even that I thought he might have committed hara kiri (suicide). He finally was sighted at Koko Head sitting on a rock down near where the waves sometimes surged up and washed fishermen away. I was asked to intervene.

I cautiously approached him and said something unimportant like, "It's a nice day, isn't it?"

Dan and I finally got around to talking about his problem,

which was, not only had he gotten his Korean girlfriend with child, but there was a Japanese girlfriend who was also pregnant. I didn't know her, not that it made any difference. What would you do, faced with this situation?

We did not solve our double oven problem for some time. However, Dan came back to work and did his usual bang-up job. The girlfriends retired to wait their terms.

Though I wondered which of the ladies Dan would bless with matrimony, or if he would marry both with a short gap in between, I did not press the matter. Dan finally came to me with the big question.

He loved both girls equally well, and could not decide which one to marry. I asked him if he had discussed this problem with his parents, thinking they would probably suggest he marry the Japanese lady. He said he had done this, and said they liked the Korean girl best.

The babies were delivered about a week apart and Dan was pleased as punch about both births. Later on, Dan married the Japanese girl.

THE LEMON QUEEN

Gladys De Coto was what you might call a "good neighbor." With a lot of growing children, we constantly ran out of things and Mrs. De Coto was always there to save the day. We even traded our Steinway baby grand piano for a Hammond upright, which was a better size for our living room. Besides, no one in our family played the piano.

The Lemon Queen of California was a good friend of Gladys's and came to Lanikai one time to visit. Instead of sending a "thank you" note when she returned home, she sent a wooden crate full of lemons. Mrs. De Coto took about a half dozen and gave us the rest – about 284 lemons.

We gave away as many lemons as we could to the neighbors and tried to talk the kids into selling glasses of lemonade from a stand outside of our yard on Mokulua Drive. However, the sandy beach and swimming on the other side of our house won out over the lemonade stand leaving us still with a lot of lemons.

From my point of view, the moral of this whole thing is if a little time were spent on research on what gifts to give to others, it could be very rewarding and not end on a sour note like this one did.

FRED KREIDT – LANIKAI

When I first knew Fred Kreidt he was a boiler inspector for the Fireman's Fund Insurance Company. I never asked him if he inspected the boilers from the inside or outside. Somehow I had a vision of him on the job dressed in overalls, a square cap and with a trowel in his hand. A third-degree Mason.

Fred and his friend Billy Worthington used to go calling on people up and down Lanikai Beach on Sunday mornings, via the ocean, in a small outboard motor boat. Generally, after a few beers, they would bid Aloha and putt-putt on to the next place.

One Saturday night at about 6 o'clock we went to a party at Fred and Rosella's. Now Fred was a very hospitable host and he always insisted on pouring his guests their first drink. There were 30 people there that night. He was not like a lot of other people I knew who poured you a big stiff one, and would give themselves a one-ouncer. He hit himself with a drink usually bigger than yours.

It was a great party, but along about 10pm we started to wonder if we had really been invited for dinner. People began to look for Fred or Rosella and found them both asleep in different bedrooms.

So some of the guests pitched in and we wound up with a fine spaghetti, salad, and garlic bread dinner.

THE FRIENDLY SONS OF ST. PATRICK

This was strictly a fun organization. The membership was quite large. There were 650 happy Irish, or want-to-be Irish, at our last big "shindig" held at the 'Ilikai Hotel.

I was president-elect and the banquet chairman in 1964. We started planning our March 17th party on the first Monday after New Year's, and each Monday thereafter, until our big event. There were chairmen for everything we could think of.

Desmond Stanley was chief of protocol, there was an assistant chief of protocol. I could go on and on. Alex Castro was a key member of this group. He changed his name to "O'Castro" for the event and passed out a treatise proving, irrefutably, that Saint Patrick was from Portugal.

President Kennedy had appointed 16 Assistant U.S. Attorneys for Hawai'i, most of them Irishmen from Boston.

One of these visiting Irishmen, supposedly close to the political system in Honolulu, suggested that rather than sneaking out on the night of the 16th of March to paint green down the centerline of Kalākaua Avenue, we get legal permission from the County's Board of Supervisors to do the painting. The supervisors were local Japanese and, not feeling the same camaraderie the rest of us "Irish" felt, they turned the idea down cold. From what happened next, it would appear that the Honolulu Police Department was tipped off.

On the night of March 16, when things had quieted down in Waikīkī, a group of our younger, and more active members gathered together for the traditional, annual paint job. They began obliterating the white median stripe down Kalākaua Avenue, from the Diamond Head end, painting it a beautiful Irish green color. About a third of the way down the avenue toward the Kapiʻolani Boulevard goal line, they decided it was time to take a break. Besides, one got dizzy leaning out over the tailgate of a station wagon. So, they gathered in a small bar that was still open, and revived themselves with the waters of the establishment.

Unbeknownst to our group of patriots, another group had begun to paint over the median strip farther down Kalākaua. They were using a sacrilegious pink paint when they were captured by the local police. Like our local politicians, they did not know pink was not "our" color. When our gang, farther up Kalākaua Avenue toward the park were sufficiently revived, they began painting again. They painted over both white and pink and finished the job just before dawn.

Prior to all this, the ladies auxiliary had been busy repairing our large, about 10' x 20', silk Irish flag. It was green with a large gold harp right in the center of it, and pretty well moth-eaten. Governor McCarthy, one of Hawaiʻi's earlier appointed governors, had flown this flag at ʻIolani Palace.

Many other preparations were made prior to March 17. Invitations were sent to President de Valera of Ireland, the Mayors of Dublin and Boston, Cardinal Spellman in New York, and many others. Aer Lingus (Irish Airways) and Pan American both agreed to send stewardesses of Irish descent to our party. Arrangements were made to have small Irish flags, green balloons, streamers, and confetti, in the right color, for the party. Permission had been received from the ʻIlikai Hotel banquet manager, Gordon Boeder, allowing the Friendly Sons to put green dye in the fountains at the ʻIlikai Hotel entrance and the fountain in the courtyard where the party was to be held.

One of our committee brothers arranged to have a large order of real live Irish shamrocks flown in free. He thought our wives, "the little darlin's" would be happy to plant them in tiny little green plastic thimbles, to use as place favors at the dinner table. Fortunately, the committee decided that although their wives were little darlin's all right, the last thing we could expect them to do was plant tiny little shamrocks in tiny little thimbles.

We wanted to have miniature bottles of Jameson's Irish Whiskey (authentic ethnic) as favors, but could not acquire them free. Therefore, we settled on little bottles of Bushmill's Irish Whiskey, courtesy of the Johnson & Buscher Beverage Company.

About one week before our big party, the AFL-CIO wrote us a letter saying they were going on strike against the 'Ilikai Hotel. They pointed to our Irish heritage and its support of labor unions down through the years, etc., etc. After very careful consideration we decided it would be very hard to change course and pick another place for the banquet. We had other, not so valid, reasons for not accepting Union President, Arthur Rutledge's plea. So, arrangements were made for people who did not wish to cross the picket line to enter the hotel through a small door on the beach side. Six hundred and fifty loyal Irish supporters had sent in their money for this most gala event.

I had discussed with banquet manager Boeder the possibility of opening up a couple of bars for a free cocktail hour before the party. I pointed out that, as he well knew, no one ever showed up at social events on time. He agreed.

The banquet was scheduled to start at 6:30pm, and free booze was to be served from 6 to 7pm. At 6pm 600 people showed up.

It was certainly a marvelous party. A number of elderly Irish, mostly widows, were there, and we all really tripped the light fantastic. Governor Bill Quinn sang "When Irish Eyes Are Smiling" and a few other songs before he wound up dancing in a fountain laced with green dye.

It was quite the formal affair for Honolulu, with some, including Bill Quinn, dressed in tails, although most wore dinner jackets with green bow ties. Naturally, green evening gowns were prominent amongst the ladies.

An Aer Lingus stewardess read us messages from the Mayor of Dublin and the head of her airline and a Pan Am stewardess sang a couple of songs in Gaelic.

Many telegrams were received wishing our banquet success, and even the pickets outside the hotel added to the flavor of things. Persons obviously not of Irish descent were carrying the signs condemning the Friendly Sons of St. Patrick, therefore, in our eyes at least, the picket line was not considered authentic.

The day after the party I felt a little embarrassed about the free cocktail hour and phoned Gordon Boeder to apologize. Before I could say anything, he said how happy he was about our party, and if we signed up for next year he would give us something better than corned beef. I asked him how the bar had made out, and he reported that our paid drinks averaged over eight per person.

Two of our members who died during the year I was president-elect asked to be buried with shillelaghs. Neither owned shillelaghs. However, we were lucky enough to "borrow" them. If any of you out there want something special for your burials, please have whatever it is handy when you die.

Erin go bragh!

A Toast to a Marlin

One day while trolling for fish off Mokumanu, O'ahu, Bobby Silverman and Tom Prentice hooked onto a fair sized marlin. The ocean was quite rough that day so Bobby, who was driving the boat said, "Don't waste any time with that buggah, just crank him in."

So Tom quietly grabbed the bending pole, sat himself down in the fighting chair all in one motion, and began to reel in the fighting fish.

The marlin jumped out of the water just once and then swam in toward the stern of the boat with hardly any effort on the part of the fisherman. You see, he had been foul-hooked in the eye, a very tender place. He put up no fight at all and, and in about 10 minutes Tom had reeled the marlin up to the stern of the boat.

Then Bobby, gaff in hand, waited until the marlin was close enough so that he could grab the leader wire and haul him up, gaff him, and bring him up over the transom and into the boat.

But this baby was "green" and as he was being pulled in over the transom the hook shook loose from his eye and it was then that he came to life twisting, turning and thrashing all over the boat.

Tom and Bobby tried to subdue him with everything they could find and finally, with both of them sitting on the marlin, he seemed to give up the ghost. But not quite!

With a sudden flick of his beautiful head, he was able to plunge his long, hard bill right through Bobby's throat - all the way.

Both men were able to pull the marlin's spear back out of Silverman's throat and then Tom revved up the engine and headed the boat home to the dock at the Kāne'ohe Yacht Club.

They noticed that there was not too much blood oozing from the two holes in Bobby's neck, so as a precautionary measure, and to ward off infection, they thought it a good idea to saturate his throat inside and out with alcohol. This was accomplished by mixing up a large batch of vodka martinis.

Bobby said that it didn't hurt too much to swallow or speak, so they became more and more pleased with their antidote.

However, much later at Castle Hospital, an emergency room doctor told them that Bobby was very lucky to be alive as the wound through his neck was only a quarter of an inch away from his carotid artery.

Pareau Sailing at Lanikai, O'ahu

We used to see and do a lot of things at the beach at Lanikai come Sunday. Lobsters could be reached under coral heads, in about six feet of water, using a face mask and a white cotton glove. Sometimes we motored over to Mokulua Island for the day with tuna sandwiches and a bottle of Tokay. Some fun!

Sailboating and water-skiing were popular sports and digging crabs out of their holes in the sand was fun for the little ones and the dogs. Once in a while something memorable would happen like the day when Olivia, clad only in a pareau, decided to water-ski behind a fairly slow outboard motor boat. As the ski boat towed Olivia slowly along the shore about 25 feet out, the knot holding her pareau loosened and her left boob popped out. Then, while she struggled to hold on to the towrope and at the same time re-cover her chest, the right one popped out. This left and then right scenario repeated itself several times before Olivia said, 'Oh, what the hell' to herself, and let go of the ski rope, settling into the water in order to use both hands to straighten things out.

A Burial at Sea – Lanikai

When John's mother died, her ashes were sent back from New York to be spread in the ocean off Lanikai. The occasion called for a farewell service ashore prior to boarding John's double-ended motor lifeboat for the trip to sea.

It was a fine service after which the guests all piled aboard the boat to sail off for a final farewell toast to John's mother and the scattering of her ashes. Unfortunately, either the boat or the wind shifted at the last moment, and as the ashes were being spread out over the waters, they blew back into the boat and onto the people.

As Fuzzy told me later, the ashes were greasy and stuck on the boat, onto the people, and just everything.

MOLOKA'I TO O'AHU CANOE RACE

About 50 years ago I was on the Aukaka, the committee boat for the Kamehameha Day canoe race from Moloka'i to O'ahu. The official radio announcer, a doctor and nurse, plus various other people were aboard. After a fine lū'au the night before the event, we went to sleep under the kiawe trees near the beach, and woke up to a dew-laden dawn and began to make our way to the canoes.

Two dear little old Hawaiian ladies were sitting on a wall right next to the beach and were laughing, rocking back and forth, and having a great time passing a pint of whiskey to each other. As we passed them, someone cried, "Hey Titas, show us your pearly toots."

As race time drew near, crews started pushing their canoes off the beach and into the waves. It was quite rough that day, and several canoes swamped as they tried to make it off the beach through the huge waves breaking on shore. All finally made it out to the starting line. Supporting crews in auxiliary boats and spectator boats milled around waiting for the race to begin.

Aboard the Aukaka, everyone was in a jovial mood, particularly the doctor, nurse, and the KGU radio announcer. The party atmosphere did not last long, however. Once we were under way, the doctor turned green and the radio announcer couldn't announce. It was very rough in the channel that day. Dave Nottage, skipper of the Aukaka, took over the radio announcer's job, reporting the status of the race to listeners around the islands, and fortunately, none of the paddlers got sick enough to require the services of "Dr. Greenface."

The race itself would have been more interesting viewed from a helicopter. As it was, the ocean swells were so high you rarely caught sight of the canoes.

Finally, a number of hours later, all boats, canoes, and paddlers arrived safely on the beach at Waikīkī --I think!'

Hawai'i

The Pu'uwa'awa'a Death March

Parker Ranch had several thousand acres of fairly level potential grazing land for its cattle, but it was full of cactus. The cactus was a good water source for cattle but poor in nutrients, so the ranch decided to get rid of it.

Two different types of cactus-eating aphids were introduced and soon the cactus began to disappear. In fact, since ants carried the cactus-destroying aphids around, the plants began to grow only in widely separated clumps.

So widely spread were they that the cowboys had to take diseased sections of the cactus and wipe more aphid-infected plants on the few good remaining cactus plants.

Right next door to Parker Ranch on the South Kona side was the extremely rocky Pu'uwa'awa'a Ranch land, loaded with cactus, which was the source of both food and water for much of Pu'uwa'awa'a cattle. The aphids were not aware of the boundaries between the ranches, and went right to work on the yummy cactus found on Pu'uwa'awa'a Ranch.

It was not long before most of the Pu'uwa'awa'a cactus was eradicated. Then along came a big drought in the area and the cattles' source of water, the cactus, was gone.

Several miles below the Belt Highway in South Kohala is Kīholo. Fresh spring water bubbles forth in the ocean just off the beach there, and for many years it was used as a drinking fountain for cattle.

Faced with a severe drought that wouldn't let up, the cattle began to die from the lack of water; water the cactus plants used to furnish. The manager of the Pu'uwa'awa'a ranch decided to drive the animals down to water, so they were herded down from way up mauka across the Belt Highway to Kīholo.

You might ask, why not truck them down? The answer to that is there was no Queen Ka'ahumanu Highway in those days, just trails over very rocky a'a lava.

Because a large number of the cattle died on the way

down, many along the Belt Highway, the descriptive name "The Pu'uwa'awa'a Death March" was given to this episode.

KAMUELA

Thirty to 40 years ago, Kamuela, known by some as Waimea, was really just a cow town. At that time, Parker Ranch owner Richard Smart was beginning to rebuild the town by remodeling ranch houses, giving them a Victorian look. Back then it was quite normal to see cowboys riding horses around town, and without the Queen Ka'ahumanu Highway and resort hotels bringing in tourists, Kamuela was a very provincial village where everybody knew each other.

I believe it was in 1959 that I stood at the main intersection in town and watched the Kamehameha Day parade go by. It took all of about 15 minutes with lots of cowboys and girls on horseback led by the grand marshal in the back seat of an open touring car. The grand marshal that year was Eben Low, an ancient haole (white) ex-cowpoke.

More than 50 years prior, Eben, claiming authority from Sam Parker, was known to have stormed into Parker Ranch Manager A.W. Carter's office with a 45 revolver to take over the ranch. Carter remained calm and told Eban that Sam only owned half of the ranch, and that Carter's ward, Thelma Parker, owned the other half and Carter intended to protect it. Thelma had owned her half of the ranch upon her father, John Parker III's death in 1894.

After many legal battles, Carter bought Sam Parker's half of the ranch for $600,000 for Thelma Parker, who then owned the ranch outright in 1906 at the age of 12. She later became the mother of Richard Smart, but both she and her husband died at very young ages, leaving Richard to be raised by his grandmother, Elizabeth Jane Dowsett Parker (Aunt Tootsie).

It was A W. Carter who made the Parker Ranch famous. He bought, consolidated, and leased property, making the ranch into the largest privately owned ranch in America.

There were a lot of interesting people living in Kamuela a few decades ago. The Purdy brothers, for example, were famous Hawaiian cowboys in the early days, winning everything in sight at both local and U.S. Mainland rodeos. They paved a path of glory at the Calgary Stampede in Canada one year, thereby contributing greatly to the honor and prestige of Hawai'i's horsemanship.

One brother came back from the rodeo circuit to Maui to work at the 'Ulupalakua Ranch, and the other brother settled down at the Parker Ranch in Kamuela. I never saw the Kamuela Purdy when he was not on his horse, a very large dark-brown job. Purdy himself always wore dark western clothes, including a large black cowboy hat. An ominous-looking hombre, to say the least, but he always sat ramrod-straight, glued to his saddle, as he trotted around town.

The leather saddlery shop, the stables where the thoroughbred horses were kept, and the breaking corral were always interesting places to visit at the ranch. A favorite crossbreed found at Parker Ranch at that time was between a percheron stud and a palomino mare. This produced a beautiful taffy-colored animal with a slightly lighter-colored mane and tail. But more importantly, the mixture also produced a horse with stronger legs and larger hooves than a palomino's. This was good for stability on the loose lava terrain on the Big Island.

The horse-breaking team of cowboys were about the toughest bunch of guys you would ever want to meet, or I should say, would never want to meet. A Mr. Maertens was the head of the group when I lived in Kamuela (Waimea), and to me, he looked just like one of the bad guys you might see in a Western movie. He was a short, bandy-legged man who probably shaved only on Sundays, and whenever I saw him, he had on an old beat-up cowboy hat that had been stamped on many times by the horses he was breaking.

The Parker Ranch horses were never 100 percent broken in. They usually remained docile while having reins and saddle put on, but when being boarded by a rider, Parker Ranch horses would give one substantial buck. This built-in idiosyncrasy on the part of the horse woke up the cowboy and let him know he had better mind his P's and Q's.

Other ranch horses had their "not quite broken" built-in quirks. On Kapapala Ranch, up toward the volcano, the horses shook and bobbed their heads vigorously when you tried to put on the reins, and horses at another ranch always seemed to turn their heads to try to bite you as you mounted. When this happened, the rider was supposed to kick the horse on the side of its head. Thus, both horse and rider were trained to give and take a little. If you didn't kick the horse after he tried to nip you, he was master for the day, and tried to rub you off his back going around fence posts or under low tree branches.

Kamehameha's Feathered Capes

King Kamehameha, the conqueror of the islands, had a very large collection of brightly colored feather capes. They were given to the Kahele family on the Big Island of Hawai'i to hide and protect.

I remember a few times, at Johnny Spencer's Steak House in Kona, we asked the last surviving member of the Kahele clan, Alice Kahele I think her name was, to tell us where the capes were stored. Not even with the aid of John Barleycorn would she divulge the secret.

I think the location of the secret hiding place must have been passed on to another guardian. Some years later, Jim Humpert described flying his airplane over a barren stretch of lava toward Kohala from Kona, and seeing a man spreading out a dozen or more beautiful feathered capes in the sun.

He said although he tried several times, he was never able to find the spot by hiking in on the ground, or by trying to find it by air again.

Prior to the Ecology Craze in West Hawai'i

Dick Frazier, manager of Honoka'a Sugar Company, would pick me up in Kamuela some Friday afternoons, and together we would ride to Kona for the weekend. In those days, we had only the narrow, unimproved, Belt Road to drive on, taking over an hour to reach Kona.

Our main goal during the drive was to finish a case of beer before we got to Kailua. We usually stopped first at Wakayama's Kamuela Liquor Store for our beer, since we got ten percent off because of our frequent purchases there. When pau (finished) with a can of beer, we would toss it out of the jeep on the lava rocks to rust away in a matter of time. You see, we added valuable minerals to the soil this way.

Nowadays you wouldn't do this, because the cans are aluminum and don't break down like steel. Then, too, we have become brainwashed on the subject of litter.

Also, and most importantly, Dick's wife and mine both later became presidents of the Kona Outdoor Circle.

THE CLERK OF THE WORKS

There was a time when the title of "clerk" was important. I guess like a lot of other job titles, "garbage man" for example, it sounds a little demeaning to this generation.

Kawaihae Harbor was dredged out so that Kohala and the Theo H. Davies plantations, Honoka'a and Hāmākua, could store and ship their bulk sugar and molasses more cheaply than shipping it through Hilo. Kawaihae Terminals were built by Castle & Cooke and Davies, who were agents for these sugar companies at the time. Union Oil Company also built a petroleum tank farm at Kawaihae, which was managed by Kawaihae Terminals.

Early in 1959, I was named manager of the facility, and so visited the area frequently during construction. When the facility was about three fifths completed, our clerk of the works died, and Castle & Cooke decided I should take over as clerk of the works, managing the contractors building the facility.

When I said, "But I'm not an engineer," to Fred Simpich, Jr., who was my boss at Castle & Cooke, he replied, "We know that, but your father is."

When the plant was completed a dedication ceremony was held with many big shots in attendance. Governor Bill Quinn, U.S. Representative Mike Kerwan, Chairman of the House Ways and Means Committee, Castle & Cooke and Davies VIP's, etc., etc.

The conveyor belts all worked perfectly when I pressed the "start" button. Whew!.

THE 29 HAND

It is very hot in Kawaihae. Forty five years ago we used to have our brown bag lunches in the air-conditioned Kawaihae Terminal office. At the time, that office sported the only air conditioner in Kawaihae.

Three of us generally had lunch together. There was Marge Kanahele, our capable secretary, Alcy D. "Shorty" Johnson (now a member of the North Hawai'i Rotary Club), and myself.

One day at lunchtime, a man from the NLRB (National Labor Relations Board) showed up and told Marge she should go away from the office to eat her lunch. Marge gave him an incredulous look and retorted, "Do you think I'm crazy?" Why would I go out in 90-degree heat to have my lunch?" NLRB, having done its job, left us for the day, and Shorty and I resumed our cribbage game.

Believe it or not, on that very day, Shorty Johnson was dealt a 29 hand. That is, he held three fives and a jack, with the fourth five of the same suit as the jack in his hand being cut.

I have played cribbage more than frequently since 1941, and I have never had a 29 hand. I held a 28 hand once during a cribbage tournament on Kaua'i, but never ever a 29.

THE KONA STEAK HOUSE

The Kona Steak House was the best place to go in Kailua-Kona in the '50's and '60's. A lively crowd of your local friends could be found there. It was informal, with shoes and T-shirts optional.

It was Johnny Spencer's Steak House at first. He became rich and famous in the '50s, sort of like Don Ho, and left the sunny isles to go to the mainland where the real money hangs out. Other owners followed, like Helen and Lynn Watt, with Chris and Gene Bergman as managers, waitress and bartenders.

They only served steak and lobster, which was kept under refrigeration until ordered. Nothing to throw away or waste. Gene was from Hoboken, N.J., but was really a reincarnation of a Tahitian god. Besides being bartender, he was sometimes chef when Bruno didn't show up.

Later there was Freddie, a very friendly piano player, who had retired from Harry Owens' orchestra. After the first verse of any song, Freddie played "How Dry I Am," and a drink would always appear for him. A good salesman for the club.

Where was the Steak House you might ask? It was tucked away, in back of the small triangular park, just past the little stores next to Moku'aikaua Church. Right next door was Emma's little sundry store and lei shop.

Auwe (alas), the Steak House is no more, and you must wear shoes in all Kona restaurants now. And too, with everybody so weight-conscious, a pure steak house just couldn't make it today. Aloha 'Oe Sizzler.

DANCING AT THE KING KAM IN THE 50'S & 60'S

Once upon a time, when Lyle Guslander was running the King Kamehameha Hotel and the Old Airport was all we had to land on, we used to love to go dancing to the music of King Kam's

Hawaiian band.

Goodness gracious, this was well before they imploded the first hotel and built a new one. Next to the old hotel, behind the banyan tree, was Taniguchi's Market (now KTA), equipped with baskets that shot up on wires from the checkout area to the office upstairs, where they cashed your money or approved your checks. Amfac's Kona offices, along with their hardware store and lumberyard, were also there.

Sometimes in the evening we would go from Keauhou to the King Kam in an outboard motorboat. When we got to the shallow channel on the Kohala side of the pier, we would gun the motor and create a wave to ride in on over the coral. Then we would "stop all engines" and glide up onto the beach.

We would tie a line from the boat to a coconut tree so it wouldn't "walk" away and go dancing. Bare feet were allowed in those days.

The King Kamehameha heiau (temple) was not so splendid then, although the ali'i and kahuna (chiefs and priests), wrapped in sheets, were paddled out to it while standing up in a canoe. We swore the hotel burned their trash out there to simulate a volcano.

History According to Bill Akau

The Passing of Keōua - 1794

Keōua, a chief who earlier had attempted to make war on Kamehameha, was captured at sea just off the Place of Refuge (Pu'uhonua O Hōnaunau) by Kamehameha's lieutenants. He was driven ashore near John Young's house at Kawaihae and, according to history books, was slain with spears by Kamehameha's men.

"Not so," says Bill Akau, Kawaihae wharfinger in the early days. Bill says as Keōua was wading ashore at Kawaihae, John Young, then governor of Hawai'i for Kamehameha I, handed Ka'ahumanu, the king's favorite wife, his blunderbuss. The queen then proceeded to use Keōua for target practice. "An he wen make," Bill said. (Translated: "And he died.")

Note: With Keōua's death, Kamehameha became the undisputed king of Hawai'i.

Kamehameha vs. Lot

There were two brothers, Kamehameha and Lot. They were very large men, strong as oxen, and very competitive. The king at that time did not know which one of his sons would live long enough to become king.

One day as Kamehameha and Lot were looking over a high pali (cliff), Kamehameha suggested they solve the problem of ascending the throne by jumping off the cliff on which they were standing.

"We are both very strong, and perhaps only one of us would survive such a fall to become king," explained Kamehameha.

Lot jumped first.

BORROWED PIPI (BEEF)

An acquaintance of ours in Waimea was caught with a few head of cattle bearing the wrong brand. The judge let him off because he said he had just "borrowed" the beef to practice roping them to get himself ready for an up-coming rodeo.

ANNA PERRY-FISK

Anna Lindsay Perry-Fisk died several years ago at the age of 95. She was the "Grand Dame" of Waimea, and she gave a lot of class to that part of the Big Island. She was not only the social leader in the community, but was also the head cowboy at her ranch. She was frequently seen on her horse herding cattle from paddock to paddock in Waimea. On the days she was working her ranch, she wore a fresh lei, often akulikuli (flowers from a succulent plant), on her cowboy hat.

Every year, Anna and her husband, Lyman Perry-Fisk, went to Honolulu over New Year's and stayed in their regular suite at the Royal Hawaiian Hotel. The hotel kept trunks of Anna's "city wear" and ball gowns in storage at the hotel pending her visits to the big city.

I asked Lyman once about the origin of his hyphenated surname. He reported there was another Lyman Perry in the community where he lived who never paid his bills. Lyman was always getting blamed for the other man's debts, so he added the name "Fisk."

Anna kept a running battle going with anyone, including the U.S. Postal Department, who referred to "her" Waimea as "Kamuela." Kamuela, as you may know, translates to "Samuel" in Hawaiian, and was the given name of Samuel Parker, the owner of the huge Parker Ranch.*   Since our major islands all have Waimeas, it would have been a problem for post offices elsewhere to know where to send mail.

This, plus quite a few hard-headed citizens and Parker Ranch supporters, has kept the government from considering a name change.

Each year during the social season, Anna held a large, formal afternoon tea at the Anna Ranch, which is right next door to the former Parker Ranch manager's house. Important ladies from the Kamuela-Waimea community were invited to take shifts serving tea and coffee from opposite ends of a very long dining room table. The sterling service was beautiful, and most of the ladies wore holokūs or billowy chiffon party dresses. Many of the ladies wore large floppy hats.

Most of the men attending hovered around the back porch of the house and were well dressed too, although they still maintained some dignity with western dress, namely cowboy boots and hats. Most of the men seemed to have a problem hanging onto the dainty coffee or teacups with their big beefy hands. This, plus also trying to hold onto a plate of cookies or cake, begged for a tragedy to occur.

On another occasion, in 1961, Anna invited a large group of us to an afternoon party at her mountain house a few miles above her ranch in Waimea. It was a party to celebrate the birthday of Robert Young, who was Richard Smart's companion at the time. Richard Smart, as you may be aware, was the sole owner of the Parker Ranch.

It was a beautiful day, and many of us brave souls went for a dip in Anna's pond, which was at the foot of a pretty little waterfall. The water was as cold as ice, so for the survival of their guests, Lyman and Anna's head cowboy went to both sides of the pool leaving a bottle of Jack Daniel's. We swam from bottle to bottle.

After our brisk swim, we moved into the ranch house where we enjoyed a delicious and extensive buffet. I remember particularly well a large standing rib roast which had come from one of Anna's prime Charlet steers.

We gathered around the living room after the buffet for liqueurs and small talk. At one point Anna remarked on how wonderful it was to be able to swim in nice, fresh, clean mountain water. "Not like those people with the swimming pools in Kona, where they did things in the water," Anna exclaimed.

I felt a little defensive about that, since we had a swimming pool in Kona. "Anna," I said, tongue in cheek, "we prevent that from happening in our Kona pool by adding a chemical so if a person does something, the water turns purple all around them."

Nice party, and along with birthday cake, Anna presented the guest of honor, Robert Young, with a large pansy lei.

Some say "Kamuela" was chosen as it was the name of an early day postmaster, Samuel Spencer.

PLEASANT PHEASANT PLUCKERS

There were still a lot of pheasants in Waimea during the hunting season back in the late '50's and '60's. If you weren't hunting and had pet dogs, it was wise to keep them in the house or chained up close to the house.

This was because hunters would often "borrow" dogs they saw along the way to help in rousting out cock pheasants. At the end of the day, they would just let the dogs run loose, which in most cases was many miles from home.

Pheasants captured in the wild are not very tasty when compared with birds raised tenderly in pens one often sees "under glass" at five-star restaurants. These are tough buggahs like our wild turkeys. However, there was a good market for the feathers found around a cock pheasant's neck.

In Waimea, there were a number of dear little old ladies who, when not sewing on Hawaiian quilts, made beautiful feather leis that men liked to wear as hatbands. Very stylish, and you might say even a little macho.

The dark-blue feathers found on the Chinese pheasant were highly prized, particularly by men wanting others to know they had "made it."

But what to do with the rest of the bird? As stated before, by almost any standard the wild pheasant is generally tough and tasteless. So the "women's club" of Waimea, or some organization like that, put out a pamphlet on how to prepare and cook a pheasant.

The recipes were designed to disguise the bird. But the best way to cook pheasant I have found is to turn several birds over to the Sun Sun Lau Chinese restaurant in Hilo and have them cooked like Chinese pot roast pork (chow yuk).

Real ono (delicious). You should try.

HUNTING IS TOUGH IN THE DARK

Before the start of pheasant-hunting season in Kamuela, it seemed every time I was charcoal broiling something out in the garage, cock pheasants would show up to watch me cook. They failed to show the moment hunting season began, however.

One evening at about 7 o'clock during the hunting season, Pierre Bowman and Don Andrews from Hāwī, about 20 miles away, showed up at the house to hunt pheasants, they said with a chuckle. By the looks of things, they had had a rough day, not all of it spent hunting birds I might add. So we helped resuscitate them with kanaka (Hawaiian) highballs (bourbon and branch water) all around. At about 8 o'clock Pierre said he must call home, which he did.

"Hello, dear; we just finished hunting and should be home in about 20 minutes. No, it's not dark over here. The sun just went down."

POACHED PIPI

Although hunting on ranch land was kapu (forbidden) without permission, rather than go home pohō (empty-handed) after a long day hunting pua'a (wild pig), it was fairly common for a trespassing hunter to kill a nice range pipi (beef). The hunter would frequently take just half of the animal, bone it out, and carry the meat home in a gunny sack.

The other half of the animal would be carefully turned over, skin-side exposed, so that from a little distance away, it looked like a whole dead steer. The Hawaiian cowboy, with a lot of range to cover, often just put down in his notebook that one make (dead) pipi was observed in the mauka (mountain) section.

Cowboys were usually paid little money by a ranch, but housing, horses and "found" were provided by the ranch. The "found" was very important as it referred to the pua'a that was considered the property of ranch personnel.

Poachers sold mostly wild pig meat to Portuguese sausage makers, but substituted beef every now and then. After adding salt, garlic and red pepper to the meat and stuffing it into casings, the sausage was then smoked. I don't think anyone could tell the difference!

FRESH WATER SHRIMP

When I lived in Waimea years ago, the water passing through the streams was so fresh and pure, I don't think they ever had to use chlorine. Admittedly, the water tasted like "nails," it was so full of iron, but we knew it was good for us.

Our dog "Sully" (short for Sultan of Lanikai) stopped by his water bowl one day and jumped about three feet in the air. I went over and looked into the water, and it was teeming with shrimp about a quarter of an inch long. So much for Waimea's filter system.

A favorite pūpū of ours is fresh water 'ōpae (shrimp) that is found in the North Kona and Kohala water tunnels. These little goodies are often cooked with salt and little Hawaiian red peppers. Hot!

I recall once at a home-style rodeo at the Gomes' ranch in Kohala everyone was in cowboy clothes, eating shrimp, and drinking beer (the church always ran the beer concession). The wild cow milking and the kids' barrel racing contests were great, but what tickled me most was looking around a circle of my buddies who were drinking beer, eating shrimp and talking story, and seeing the red shrimp whiskers (feelers) hanging from their lips.

ROPE NELSON'S BOAT BLEW UP

Shortly after Rope Nelson had filled his boat's fuel tanks with diesel, it blew up. Rope was shot like a cannon through the roof of his sampan, fortunately suffering only a cut on his ear. The rest of the boat was toothpicks. The tank truck that filled the boats at the Kailua dock carried diesel in the front half and gasoline in the back half of the tank. I sometimes wonder....

"DOC" HILL

I did not know "Doc" Hill* as well as Whitey Rose and others did, but I did know him a little bit; enough to lose about 20 bucks to him playing cribbage between Hilo and Honolulu on a Hawaiian Airlines DC-3.

Another time, we played cribbage all the way at sea from Keauhou to Hilo on his haole (white) sampan, the Miss Kona. Doc enjoyed cribbage more than fishing so our lines were brought in for good once we were off Kealakekua.

Doc Hill sold eye glasses in the plantation villages in the early days. He must have carried a very large suitcase full of them, because I am told he made a fortune selling glasses in a very short time.

114

They say a plantation worker would try on different degrees of magnifying glasses until he found a suitable pair. Then, with his new glasses on, he would high-step down the road, which now appeared much closer to his feet than it actually was.

Although I suspect it may not be a 100-percent true, I was told a story about Doc when he was on a Hawaiian Airlines flight between Honolulu and Hilo that never arrived in Hilo. He was looking out of a window on his side of the plane and noticed the propeller had stopped. He poked a friend's arm across the aisle and said, "The propeller on my side has stopped going around!"

His friend looked out his window on the opposite site of the airplane, and exclaimed, "Mine has stopped too!"

Happily, the DC-3 made a safe landing in a newly harvested sugar cane field on the Hāmākua coast.

William H. "Doc" Hill was a very big industrialist on the Big Island of Hawai'i and a Hawai'i State Senator.

FALLOUT SHELTERS

We don't give fallout shelters much thought nowadays, but in the '50's and early '60's they were mighty important in Hawai'i. Some of you may even remember the fallout drills we had, and scurrying into designated shelters. Hawai'i was supposedly out of an atomic bomb's total destruction range.

We were told fallout shelters might give us a chance of survival in some sections of Hawai'i. A two-week supply of canned food and water was kept on hand in these shelters.

In Kona, just off where King Kamehameha III road is (or was), is a very large lava tube that was to house several hundred Kailua residents in case of an attack.

We still have the warning sirens throughout the islands, but today their primary use is to tell us when a tidal wave is coming.

HOLD THE PLANE FOR MICKEY SPILLANE

After World War II, Hawai'an Airlines switched from DC-3's to Convairs for flights between the islands. While the timeliness of departures improved with the new aircraft, flights were still not always on time. In fact, later in the day, delays multiplied and the Convairs would arrive and depart later and later.

115

Businessmen flying from Honolulu to the Big Island were frequently late getting home and many a wife said, "Joe, you smell like a brewery." She was right, of course, because delays, sometimes an hour or more, caused these impatient gentlemen to congregate around pitchers of beer in the airport bar located near the departure gates.

Besides just being late, planes were often delayed for other reasons. Sometimes, depending on the length of the delay, and who was aboard, they even served in-flight champagne to the passengers.

One of several memorable delays I remember was on a flight from Honolulu to Kona with a large contingent of hot, sweaty haole (white) tourists. After a delay of about an hour, we boarded the plane and taxied all the way out to the runway for takeoff, with our grumbling bunch of passengers.

The engines were revved up one at a time and then, after pausing quietly for a minute, the two engines were given full power and we were ready to speed down the runway and up into the air.

No such luck. The pilot suddenly cut everything, the engines fluttered down like a heart attack. Over a crackling speaker, he announced our flight had been called back to the passenger terminal. The airplane crawled slowly back to the terminal where the entry door was opened to let some nice, hot Honolulu air into the cabin for our passengers, who were already very hot under the collar.

Two people climbed aboard the plane, a well-dressed businessman and a very attractive young lady. It was Wendell Carlsmith with his daughter.

"Who the hell do you think you are? Do you own the airline or something?" shouted an angry passenger.

At that time Mr. Carlsmith, a prominent Hilo lawyer, did indeed own the airline.

Aloha!*

*Aloha has an important meaning here, as at the time Hawaiian Airlines had no competition.

THE FRIENDLY FOKKERS – 1960 (AT THE OLD KONA AIRPORT)

In the good old days before the King Kamehameha Hotel was imploded and the Kona Airport was right behind it, Hawaiian Airlines had switched from DC-3's to Convairs, and Aloha Airlines flew F-27's, the "Friendly Fokkers."

Several of us commuted to Kailua-Kona on weekends, and then took late Sunday evening flights back to Honolulu. These flights were usually an hour or so late. But never mind. The King Kamehameha's bar was right next door and we happily whiled away our time with mai tais and "martoonies."

Finally, we would hear the whine of our arriving F-27 or Convair two feet above the hotel's roof. Or, if the wind was the other way, Donna, Aloha's "man" at the airport, or Walter Perreira, Hawaiian's manager, would phone the bar to let us know the "Connie" or the "Friendly Fokker" was leaving for Honolulu in five minutes. We never missed a plane.

HERBERT SHIPMAN

Mr. Shipman owned a lot of land on Hawai'i Island and was also a very important, influential business leader. He had a lot to do with the Hilo Meat Company and was smart enough to sell Castle & Cooke several thousand acres of heavily forested land at Kea'au just outside of Hilo. Castle & Cooke grew macadamia nut trees and processed nuts there.

In the '50's and '60's, much of this dense forestland was unfenced and overrun with wild cattle. Big, wide, vicious horns made you think of Texas when longhorns roamed the prairie.

On the western slope of Mauna Ke'a, above Parker Ranch's Humu'ula sheep station, Mr. Shipman had a ranch house and nearby there was a large piece of land, maybe 20 acres, tightly fenced in by tall cypress trees.

Inside this corral of trees was the Shipman flower farm, and just before Easter, the Shipman ranch hands put down their branding irons and the other tools of the cowboy trade, and picked up flower shears.

They cut and packed enough daffodils for shipment to Honolulu for the Easter flower market. This was one of the wrangler jobs they didn't write home about.

THE CATTLEMAN'S ASSOCIATION

The Hawai'i Cattleman's Association was a good group to belong to, and Kawaihae Terminals joined it by providing a case of whiskey. Great jeep treks were made to inspect the various ranch operations on Hawai'i Island.

About 20 or 30 jeeps went along on these "safaris" with "oasis" stops about every half hour to cool down engines and to refresh members and guests with beer, Bloody Marys, and gin and tonics.

The ranches visited put on marvelous barbecues. I remember a trip to Billy Paris's when a whole steer was cooked on a huge outside rotisserie contraption.

One year, the local Cattleman's Association invited the California Cattleman's Association to hold joint meetings with it in Kona. Many seminars were held along with a lū'au and other social events.

A luncheon meeting at the Waiaka Lodge took place on the last day the mainland U.S. group was in Kona. Not being a full-fledged member, I was not there, and happened to run into Herman Mulder, resident manager of the Kona Inn and Waiaka Lodge, at the Union Oil station in Kailua that afternoon.

I asked Herman how the lunch was and what ranch had provided the steaks. He replied the luncheon had been very good but he had served steaks from the mainland as he felt he couldn't serve the visiting cattlemen our lousy island beef.

Later that day, I asked a friend how the lunch was, and he replied the steaks Waiaka Lodge fed them were just awful, tough as anything.

"But," he said, "we didn't dare say anything because we knew it was island beef, probably from Parker Ranch."

GIANNINI THE GOURMET

I don't know if Ray Giannini, the chemist at Kohala Sugar Co., was kidding when he said although he was from San Francisco, his father was a bootlegger and not a banker (A. P. Giannini, Bank of America founder).

Anyway, Ray was most noted and loved in North Hawai'i for his excellent homemade brandy, antipasto, and cheese. He made the first two items with the help of Tom Orlin from Honoka'a. They imported the cheese from Italy until they found out the cheese made in Wisconsin was just as good.

When Ray was the chemist at Kohala Sugar Company, he was responsible for seeing that quality raw sugar was delivered to Kawaihae for shipment to the C&H refinery at Crockett, California.

One day Dick Frazier, manager of Honoka'a Sugar Co.,

and I were visiting at the bulk sugar receiving station at Kawaihae, when he noticed some small, round, brown things in a truckload of Kohala's raw sugar being weighed in. "What is that?" Frazier questioned.

They were little balls of molasses which had stayed in the sugar. Kohala was never able to cure the problem, probably because it cost too much money. So forever after, we didn't call them molasses balls, they had become "Giannini's Balls."

GIANNINI THE WARRIOR

During World War II Ray Giannini was a tail gunner on B-17 flying missions over Burma. Ray told us the following story about one flight he was on over the Burmese jungles:

Ray was back in his bubble looking down at the forest when he heard one engine begin to sputter. This was followed by another engine which coughed a few times and quit. Then Ray says that over the intercom came, "Pilot to crew, pilot to crew, we are having engine failure, bail out now!"

Sgt. Giannini, being a good soldier, bailed out immediately, and as he floated down into the jungle under his parachute, he looked up and couldn't see any other parachutes. In fact, as he squinted some more, he saw the engines had started again, and the plane was flying off into the sunset.

Ray said he spent three miserable weeks lost in the jungle before being rescued. Fortunately the natives were friendly.

YOU CAN TALK TO MADAME PELE

Back in the '60's our fire goddess, Madame Pele, almost swallowed up Kapoho with her mantle of fiery lava. Many lost their beach homes, but the Al Stearns family did not.

Now you may think it was just luck the lava flow stopped as it reached the East, North and South corners of Al's lot (the ocean was on the West side). But perhaps it was something else.

In addition to many Christian prayers, Stearns enlisted the help of a well-known kahuna from the North Kohala district to give him a hand in holding Madame Pele back from her desire to swallow up the Stearns's hale (house).

They traveled the long way from Hāwī to Kapoho and arrived there just ahead of the oozing lava. The kahuna, dressed in an all-white mu'umu'u, shook some ginger (and possibly some animal blood) on the four corners of Al's property and, in Hawaiian, he asked Pele to please spare this good man's property, and she did!

THE CANE TASSEL

In 1959 when I joined the Hāmākua Rotary Club, we met Monday evenings at six o'clock at the Honoka'a Club Restaurant. Later we moved around the corner to another place because we were served too many meat loaf dinners, or some other reason.

All 26 members of our club were in some way involved with the sugar industry, and since many were Scottish engineers (brought in to run the sugar mills in the early days), the masthead on the club's bulletin reflected both the Scotch and the sugar influences.

Pictured at the top on each side of the "Cane Tassel" were two plaid-skirt-attired, knobby-kneed Scots, each holding a tassel-topped stalk of sugar cane.

The club was known for its excellent cribbage players, and we could hardly wait for invited speakers to finish their talks so we could get going with our cribbage games.

ROSIE CHONG'S IN KAILUA-KONA

We never got around to calling "Rosie Chong's" by its real name, Ocean View Inn, but this Big Island restaurant was a great place to take the family for Sunday night dinner.

While we were waiting for our own special dinners to come, we would unsheathe our wooden chopsticks, "sharpen" them to get rid of the splinters, and then see if we could pass an ice cube, fished out of a glass of water, all the way around the table from person to person without dropping it. This was how our kids became proficient in the use of chopsticks.

Then, the assorted dinners would come: hamburgers with mashed potatoes and gravy, hekka, sweet and sour mahimahi and other dishes, along with an extra bowl of rice and shoyu.

THE OLD DUMP

The old dump in Kailua Kona was on Palani Road behind where the fire station is today. Since there was no garbage service 30 years ago, it was socially acceptable for the best people in town to show up there.

Mongoose could also be found there in great numbers. Our boys loved the place, as it provided them with an excellent chance to practice their marksmanship. Much better than a shooting gallery, with real live expendable targets.

The little guys would heave rocks at the critters, and older boys would shoot at them with bows and sharpened arrows, BB guns, or 22's.

After all, the Vietnam War was just a few years away.

THE KAHALU'U QUEEN'S BATH

I'm sure you have heard about the pond next to the beach at Kahalu'u in Kona. Before a tidal wave in 1961, the now missing pond, known as The Queen's Bath, was much larger - oval, about 60 feet wide and 150 feet long -- and deep, with a lava-rock wall around it. The pond was quite pretty then, and it's a pity it hasn't been brought back up to snuff.

Before sand filled in the pond, it was a nice tourist attraction. Whenever we drove by the Queen's Bath with visitors back then, we used to say, "And that is the Queen's Bath. The queen was a rather large woman."

LYNN WATT'S NINE-HOLE GOLF COURSE

There was a nine-hole golf course at Keauhou Bay in the early '60's. The Clubhouse was Lynn Watt's home, and while there were no golf carts, we did have caddies and a portable two-legged bar.

The course was laid out across the street from where the Keauhou Yacht Club is and where Harry Lyons later lived. The north end of the course was where King Kamehameha III's commemorating monument is located. The south end was about where the small boat ramp can be found today.

Living-room-type golf balls with holes were used for eight of the nine holes, and a little kid or two were caddies. My handicap was so high, I was the "two-legged bar" a couple of times. The bar was generally limited to beer, Bloody Marys, gin and tonics, and cokes.

The ninth hole was the most exciting because a real live golf ball was used. You drove, or I should say chipped, the ball over the roof of the Watts' house and tried to make a hole-in-one by having the ball drop into their swimming pool rather than Keauhou Bay.

It was risky letting a high gross golfer play the last hole. Bloody Mary, anyone?

The Favorite Lure

The fishing was almost always good off of South Point on the island of Hawai'i. A little rough perhaps, but the eating fish you caught, like ono and ahi, made the long trip down from Kailua worthwhile.

One time when we were there overnight, we spent the cocktail hour, as usual, catching mempaches by lantern light off the stern of the anchored Adelante. These small fish were then mixed with miso paste and boiling water, resulting in delicious soup.

The next morning, before the sun was up, we heaved up the anchor and were on our way with five lines out. Barely had we played out the first line when, zing, we hooked our first small ahi. Almost immediately, there were fish on the other lines and we pulled in five ahi, each about five pounds. Lines were again put out and, again we only stopped the boat after hooking the fifth fish to reel them in.

We older fishermen soon became pooped, so we turned the fishing over to the kids. They had more stamina then we did and were all in good shape from the football training they got at school at H.P.A. (Hawai'i Preparatory Academy) in Kamuela. We, the elders, quickly opened up beers and shouted words of encouragement to the boys so they wouldn't quit on us.

Pretty soon, it couldn't have been more than two hours, the fish boxes were just about full with the ahi iced down. Everybody took a happy breather, sitting around either sucking on a beer or a coke, or munching on musubi.

About then, someone noticed Bobby (RL) Hinds' Kilohana about a mile away. R.L., and whomever he had on board, was waving at us so we waved back. Charlie Spinney, skipper of the Adelante, tried to raise the Kilohana on the radio to share our good fishing news with them, however the reception was so garbled, we gave up.

Then, we noticed that the American flag on the other boat was flying upside down. Naturally, this meant distress, which in this case, we all thought it meant he was out of beer. We maneuvered over close by and prepared to "pass the ammunition – a case of cold beer." We were almost stern to stern when we finally understood what R. L. and his crew, Freddie Shatthauer, were saying. They were hooked up to a huge thresher shark and needed some help with it. "The buggah has my favorite lure and I want it back," yelled R.L.

So, one of our more daring crewmen, or should I say, our most daring crewman, Don Quaintence, volunteered to jump from the stern of our boat to theirs, to give them a hand. The rear ends of both boats were going up and down in the choppy water, with no regular rhythm for "Q " to time his jump onto the stern of the Kilohana.

He jumped anyway, and missed the Kilohana, disappearing into the sea between the two boats. Talk about a hairy situation. Boats too close to each other could have squashed him, or maybe the angry shark could have attacked him.

The next thing I saw was a pair of size 14 feet shooting up out of the ocean, propelling Quaintence into standing position, wet and very white, on the deck of R.L.'s boat. This was the first time I had ever seen anybody jump feet first out of the water. As we drifted away from R.L.'s boat, we were horrified to see Freddie Shatthauer holding the shark's mouth open, with the business end of a stainless steel flying gaff wedged in the shark's mouth, while Quaintence reached in between the big shark's teeth, and happy day, worked R.L. Hinds' favorite lure loose.

DOVE HUNTING AT KAWAIHAE

A few years ago, dove hunting was terrific along the low-lying hills above Kawaihae. Flocks of the fattest birds you ever saw would zoom low over the sloping terrain in the early mornings and late afternoons.

There was a cattle feed lot situated at Puakō near Kawaihae which was supplied with truckloads of bulk corn and other feed from silos located at the port of Kawaihae.

A steady trail of grain spilled from the trucks hauling the cattle feed all the way from the port to Puakō. This provided a convenient "feed lot" for the doves.

Hunters would stand and shoot at the large flocks of plump birds as they flew by. Better marksmen like Dr. Alex Burso used small bore 22 gauge shotguns and everyone brought home plenty of meat for the dinner table. Charcoal broiled squab that had been fattened on Kawaihae corn was real ono (good)!

SWEET LEILANI RUM

The Seagram's Distilling Company began to produce rum on Maui in 1964. Since I was president of the State Chamber of Commerce then, I flew over from Honolulu for the dedication ceremonies in honor of this new industry.

Seagram's had chartered two Convairs to fly notables over to Maui and I sat next to a young fellow (then), by the name of Bronfman, who was to become president of Seagram's. In making conversation with him, I asked what the new rum would be called, and he said, "Sweet Leilani."

He followed this by telling me the name of a product was not too important. "After all," he said, "our most profitable brand of whiskey is Four Roses."

The governor of Hawai'i and many other important people from Maui attended the ceremony, which took place in an open area between the HC&S Sugar Mill and the new rum-producing plant.

The molasses was fed from HC&S into the rum plant through a small pipe after some purifying work was done, and a little sugar syrup added, since molasses produced in Hawai'i from sugar cane is practically sugarless by the time it reaches that state.

About 200 or so honored guests gathered to hear speeches and prayers ending with the cutting of a long maile lei which signified the opening of the rum plant. The governor and Maui's mayor told the throng what a marvelous economic boon this new rum plant was going to be to the economy of the Hawaiian Islands.

The speeches were rather long, so during lulls in the thing, I asked the new rum plant manager a few natural questions about the enterprise. "How many people will it take to run the plant?" I asked. "Two," he replied. "How long will you age the rum before bottling it?" I asked. "As soon as the product is made here, it will be shipped to the Mainland U.S. for further processing and bottling," he replied.

The most fun thing about the whole day was watching newly made rum drip one slow drop at a time on the plant manager's head from a loose connection in the copper ceremonial pipe above through which new rum was flowing slowly into a ceremonial cask.

He stood rigidly at attention, not moving a muscle throughout the whole procedure. I guess he could legitimately be called a "drip."

CLAIRVOYANCE ON MAUI?

So, there we were, having a quarterly meeting of the Hawai'i State Chamber of Commerce, at a new resort on Maui. It had been built with Canadian money and was very nice, in a sparse sort of way. I had learned that before a meeting the top dog, me, as president of the chamber, should check out the meeting room to make sure the microphone worked, the tables and seating were right, along with other things which might be required such as a blackboard, movie projector, etc.

Fritz Herman, head of Eastman Kodak in Hawai'i, George McLean, a director of the chamber who was also on the permanent staff of the chamber, and I went on the mission to check out these things.

What we found were three young ladies sitting in the room sipping drinks through straws. Fritz Herman, never one to be backward about anything, asked if we could buy them a drink, to which they replied in the affirmative.

After introductions I said, "And you ladies are nurses," to which they responded. "Yes! How did you know?"

Without answering, I went on to say they were from Canada. They asked with some astonishment how I knew, and again without replying, I said, "and I suppose you all graduated from the B. C. nursing school, and are from Saskatoon, Saskatchewan."

They said, "Yes, yes, but how in the world could you know?"

It happened that they left at that point, so I couldn't give them the lowdown on how I knew so much about them. So here is how I had put it "scientifically" together:

1. Apprentice nurses who came to Hawai'i from the mainland U.S. or Canada in those days were sent to the neighbor islands before being transferred into the big hospitals in Honolulu.

2. These were three white, rosy-checked young ladies who were obviously not tourists or schoolteachers.

3. The resort hotel was owned by Canadians.

4. Betty McQuaig McCoy, a childhood friend, had studied nursing at B.C. and told me it was the best nursing school in the world.

5. Fraternity brothers Mickey Packer and Jim McPhee were at U.C.L.A. on ice hockey scholarships, and both of them were from Saskatoon, Saskatchewan.

What more did I need to know!

A Minnesotan Visits Hawai'i

Cousin Bob phoned from Rochchester, Minnesota shortly after Christmas to compare the cold weather there with the warm weather here in Kona. He said he would give anything for a photo of himself swimming in the warm ocean in Hawai'i on New Year's day.

So, we invited him to visit us and he arrived in Kona a few days before December 31st. He stepped off the airplane wearing a bright orange and green aloha shirt, yellow checked polyester trousers, and a pork pie hat. He said he could hardly wait for New Year's day for a photo of himself swimming in the warm Pacific. He said he wanted it to show to the Mayor of Rochchester, a close personal friend.

At Kahalu'u Beach on New Year's morning, Bob waded into the water, stopping to face the camera with the water slightly above his ankles. "Go ahead, Bob, go out and swim around," I exclaimed. "This is as far as I'm going," retorted Bob, as he made his way back to the beach.

We toured Hawai'i Island and I got the impression Cousin Bob was not a true believer. "It's about 90 miles to the Volcano House," I'd tell him, to which he would reply, "Is that so?"

"Mauna Ke'a is almost 14,000 feet high," I'd say, and he would follow with, "Is that so?"

Every statement I made was followed by "Is that so?" When Cousin Bob was leaving Kona to head back to the winter cold of Minnesota, I said, "I hope the photograph of you in the warm Kona ocean will wow them when you get home," and he replied, "You better believe it."

I answered, "Is that so?"

Kapu (Taboo)

In the old days private property was respected in Hawai'i. Usually, the only sign one saw on house lots, ranches, and farmland, was a small one that read "kapu."

Then in the '60's a new kind of person started to invade our islands. They were called "hippies." Many members of this tribe of hippies did not respect personal property, and mango, papaya, banana and avocado trees were often ruthlessly stripped of their fruit.

Gradually our kapu signs, which meant "keep out," disappeared. People thought perhaps these mainland strangers did not understand kapu, so new signs were put out which read "Keep Out," "No Trespassing," "Private Property," or "Beware of Dog." Sadly, the lack of consideration for private property did not change with the new signs.

While there aren't many hippies in Hawai'i today, the habit of trespassing is still with us. Some hippies (others also) turned to private enterprise, i.e. growing pakalolo (marijuana), although they often grow it on someone else's property.

Perhaps the restored Hawaiian monarchy will take care of problems such as this and will return things to the good old days of kapu.

GOAT HUNTING IN KA'U

Hunting wild goats in the rugged lava of the Ka'u desert was like being in a shooting gallery waiting for the next tin soldier, or duck, to pop up.

One weekend the boys went off in a jeep for an overnight trip of hunting and fishing. They weren't lucky in the fishing department, but they did manage to get five goats, including one they ran over. When we asked what they did with the goats, they replied they had traded them at the Na'alehu Restaurant for milk shakes.

For the next two weeks at the restaurant they served a lot of "lamb" stew and "lamb" curry.

KALALAU VALLEY

There has always been a hermit of Kalalau Valley. In actual fact, there have been many hermits there, but "the hermit" sounds more romantic.

This valley is tucked away from civilization on the island of Kaua'i. You reached it by boat until modern conveniences like helicopters came along to provide an easier access to the place.

The Tom Prentice family from O'ahu 'coptered over there a few years ago for a week's vacation and had a wonderful time roughing it. There was one problem, though: the hermit of Kalalau Valley showed up NAKED for a visit.

With three young girls in the family, Tom thought this was going a bit far, so he asked the hermit if he would mind putting something on in deference to his little girls. Hermit complied, showing up now and then with a towel wrapped around his waist.

As prearranged, at the end of the week a helicopter arrived and picked up the Prentices to carry them back to civilization. As they rose in the air, the hermit of Kalalau showed up to wave good-bye.

You guessed it. . . he waved to them with his towel.

What is a Minority?

Forty years ago, I was an employee of a large Hawaiian company that was investigated by the National Labor Relations Board for its alleged anti-minority hiring practices.

The company proved that 35 percent of its current employees were members of minority groups. We had Japanese, Chinese, Portuguese, Puerto Ricans, Hawaiians and other minorities working for us.

The head of the NLRB's investigating team said, "We are not talking about those minorities. You must have at least 14 percent of the one minority we are talking about on your payroll. He went on to say that if this situation were not corrected, the company would not be eligible for further U.S. Government business.

Back in 1935, I applied for Christmas vacation work at two different American-Japanese stores in Honolulu. At both stores, I was told, "We won't hire you, you're a haole!"

In 1935, haoles were a minority in Hawai'i.

The Second Coming?

Chuck Watson is a very talented artist. He was head of construction for Dillingham, and at one time received quite a bit of notoriety for his "topping off" party held on the roof of the revolving restaurant atop the 25-story Ala Moana building. Lots of beer! Empty cans – I don't believe they were bottles – were thrown off the roof, nearly striking a policeman below who had been called to the scene because of the noise.

On the other hand, Watson's artwork in metal and in stone is fabulous. What an artist! The following is according to my good friend Tom Prentice: The Watson home and guesthouse were perched on a peak overlooking Lanikai, with the Mokulua Islands and the blue Pacific beyond. The guesthouse was rented to a religious group who were sort of on the quiet side.

Pony Watson, Chuck's wife, had taken a trip to the mainland,

and this left Chuck with a lot of time to indulge in his favorite sport, poker. He invited some of his friends in, and for several days they had quite a card bang.

What they didn't know, was that during this time something unusual was going on next door in the guesthouse. It seems the head priest of the religious order was an avid parasailor, but had suffered a rather severe accident when he sailed off a cliff at Makapu'u.

The priest's followers brought him back to their "church" (Chuck's guesthouse), and attempted to revive him. He was dead, however, but they thought he might come back to life in about three days if they tied him to a cross. So after propping him upright, the congregation left.

Later, either someone complained or someone ratted, because the police arrived and found the body in bad condition in the guesthouse. Seeing and smelling cigar smoke coming out of Chuck's place, and hearing loud voices and laughter, along with the clinking of glasses, they surrounded the house (SWAT-team style) and burst in, arresting all present.

Chuck and his buddies had quite a time explaining they were not involved in the happenings next door.

Two-Step Beach

Two-Step Beach is my name for a large flat area of pāhoehoe (smooth) lava which juts out into the ocean at Hōnaunau Bay, just north of the Place of Refuge historic park.

Kona dive-shop students practice scuba diving in the bay. There is a nice concrete ramp for launching fishing boats on the south side of the flat lava rock. The beach is quite small and, unlike the song, young rather than old Hawaiians play on it.

Two Step provides easy access into the water for swimmers, snorkelers, and scuba divers. The first step is about two feet down to another perfectly formed wide step. A person can sit comfortably on the top step to put on his fins and mask, and then he can just float off the second, or bottom step, into the sea

The ocean is about eight feet deep there, and then gets gradually deeper and deeper. Tropical fish such as parrot fish and angelfish are plentiful, and it is a beautiful place to snorkel and dive.

THE GREENBANK ESTATE

John Dowie, a very tall, thin, good-looking, red-haired fellow, contacted Nancy (my wife) during her reign as president of the Kona Outdoor Circle (KOC) to ask for help in identifying the various flora found at the Greenbank Estate property in North Kohala

The Greenbank property comprises about 50 acres of tropical plants; many planted in the late 1800's through the efforts of Dr. Wight and his family who arrived in Māhukona, North Kohala when they were shipwrecked in 1850.

Naturally, the KOC was interested in inspecting the property and helping Mr. Dowie in the development of his botanical garden plans. A preliminary expedition was formed and a small group of Outdoor Circlers, including county agent, Norman Bezona of the Agricultural Extension Service, drove over to the Greenbank Estate, the entrance of which is just past the Chinese temple in North Kohala on the way to Pololū Valley.

We drove from Kona with Kathy and Bill Martin in their new 4-wheel drive Cherokee. I commented on the comfortable ride we were having and mentioned that my son Charlie had the same kind of car, but that he had found it did not climb the hills in San Francisco too well. Bill retorted his new Cherokee had plenty of power, more than his "Caddie." However, I did notice while driving along, Bill drove the car in a low, rather than high gear, all the way to Kohala and back.

As we entered the property I saw, in an open area of about 200 by 100 feet, a couple dozen small A-frame huts about two-feet high with beautifully feathered fighting cocks tethered to each one. "Ah ha," I said, "Mr. Dowie, looks like a real sports fan!"

As soon as we met tall, good-looking John Dowie, Nancy asked him if he was using the birds for cock-fighting. Dowie answered, "Oh, no. I have them just for pets because they are so beautiful."

The estate was loaded with tall trees and hundreds of varieties of tropical plants. A huge ironwood tree (Australian native) was supposed to be the first ironwood brought to Hawai'i. Although much of the land was overgrown with staghorn fern, an island pest which is almost impossible to walk through, we could see at one time the place had been a gorgeous garden spot.

There were about four mainland, retired hippies working for Mr. Dowie to clear brush away, but it was quite obvious they were the non-professional variety of gardeners.

As Norman Bezona pointed out to Dowie, some under-growth is necessary for the proper maintenance of a forest. Without it, Norman said, erosion of the earth occurs and tree roots become bare and the trees topple over.

We hiked down into a high forest of trees and ferns, passing several terraces which had held water for taro cultivation at a time prior to Dr. Wight's arrival. We crossed a small stream, stepping from rock to rock, and entered into a most interesting graveyard surrounded by an ancient wrought-iron fence. This was the burial site for the Wights and many of their descendants – all except one! According to John Dowie, one of the Wight children ran off and married a native Hawaiian. This was a "no-no" to Dr. Wight, although it certainly was not to haoles, before and after Dr. Wight.

We looked at all of the gravestones, about a dozen or more, very old, and many of them tilted this way and that. The most pictur-esque was a gravestone found at the base of a tall and very old kapok tree. High roots surged down from the tree and encircled the grave like a pair of large arms. The gravestone stood as straight up as the day it had been set there, which was amazing, in view of the more than 100 years it had been there in the jungle.

On the way back we used a "Hawaiian escalator" to ride up a muddy embankment. This escalator was made by using a large wooden block and tackle arrangement, fastened to a tree trunk at the top of the embankment, with a heavy rope woven through it. We grabbed onto this line, one at a time, and the most stalwart of the Dowie hippie "worker bees" heaved on the rope from the bottom of the hill, giving us an easy, though slippery, walk to the top.

After our hike, we gathered at our starting point at the top of the property where Mr. Dowie gave us a great picnic lunch of ham, baked beans and potato salad, which we washed down with very nice Sauvignon blanc.

Dowie told us much of what he had learned of the history of the area, and showed us where the old Wight home had been. He said the house was haunted and many unusual things had happened in it. "The place would rattle and shake at night," he told us.

He said that in knocking the place down, a heavy bulldozer which had been left there overnight was found the next day mysteri-ously turned over on its side. Spooky, yes?

The inspection party thought the place was so interesting

from the historical and flora points of view that we arranged to have a Kona Outdoor Circle outing there a few months later. A busload of KOC members, Bloody Marys and all, had a great day and wished Mr. Dowie well in his venture to turn the Greenbank Estate into a botanical and historical garden.

It was with some shock about a year later we read in the local press that the U.S. Federal Government had seized the property. The story in the paper said John Dowie had purchased the property with drug-related money. The whereabouts of Mr. Dowie were unknown, although it was assumed he had fled the country.

Too bad, I somehow do not think of Dowie as a bad person, and hope some day he will come back to face the music.

CLARISSA

The last time Auntie Es came to Kona from Osage, Iowa, she brought along Clarissa, an old pal of hers. I must say the two of them had a dandy time of it here in Kona.

Clarissa was the widow of a Lutheran minister, so for awhile our household was blessed with a good share of religion. Our guest had been in charge of the church choir back in Osage, and on Sundays, at different churches here in Kona, we stood in awe as she belted out hymns. I tell you, choirs had to be on their toes to keep from being drowned out by this lady.

Another change in our normal laid-back way of life here in Kona was the blessing Clarissa gave before each of our daily meals. We would hold hands, bow our heads, and close our eyes as we listened to her give thanks, and what not, to the Lord. Initially, Clarissa's blessings were short and sweet, but they grew longer and longer as she observed our many human transgressions. The last night she and Auntie Es were here, we had a leg of lamb for dinner, and as usual, Clarissa asked if she could give the blessing. Expecting this to be a very long parting shot, I gazed at the steaming food and said, "Of course, Clarissa, but I do hope it can be a short one." It was.

Auntie Es and Clarissa went to Honolulu for three or four days to see the sights. They had a great time going to all of the tourist places and visiting as many different churches as time permitted.

One day they got into a long line of "worshippers" going into a Buddhist temple. When they were inside, they found they had nestled into a line of mourners attending a feast following a funeral. They were encouraged to partake of the food, and as Auntie Es told us later, "although the food was Oriental, it was quite delicious!"

THE PUNAHOU CLASS OF 1939 REUNION

I looked forward to my 65th high school class reunion. The last one I had gone to was about 15 years prior to that. It was nice to see everybody, although the group was rather small. The girls (are you listening, ladies?) all looked amazingly young and beautiful but most of the guys looked a lot older than I had expected.

I guess the men looked older because of so many years of hard work. I think the women were better preserved because, with a few exceptions, women in our generation were not expected to work and had lots of time to keep themselves looking attractive.

The lū'au on Alexander Field is awfully good and the thing I like about it most is that when you reach our age, we are seated and served and do not have to stand in a long line like the younger graduates. As you might expect, many in our class even have had grandchildren that have graduated from Punahou.

The people in the class of '39 ran the gamut, from good to poor grades, and, from those who went to work right after high school, to those who accumulated many graduate degrees. The wealthiest person in the class was Charlie Gates, Jr.. At one point Forbes listed him as one of the 400 wealthiest Americans with $1.3 billion. But, regardless of station, I think we are all a happy and successful bunch of people.

At a party before reunion a few years ago Chokie Denison exclaimed, "Look at George over there, talking to the girls as usual."

I hope at our next reunion someone says, "look at George over there, talking to the girls." I know the girls will all still look young and beautiful.

LOCAL ENGLISH IS TOO AMERICAN NOW

The influence of the New England missionary teachers who taught the English language in Hawai'i was passed all the way down to my generation in the '30's.

Although the Boston-like accents were somewhat modulated by the softer sounds of the Hawaiian language, there was no give as far as grammar was concerned. Perhaps a little "caning" kept the older generations in line.

"Ain't" was never heard, and anyone saying, "it don't"

instead of "it doesn't" would not be welcomed at home again. A softer-than-Boston "mothah, fathah, sistah and brothah" was fine, and "cahn't" was more normal than "can't."

There was such fear attached to when you should use the objective "me" instead of "I," that the word "me" was almost completely eliminated from our vocabulary.

During the '20's and '30's a few tried to get away from the broad "a" and words such as "idea" became "idear." Eventually, during and after World War II, Americanized English gradually took over, and I'll have to admit the youth today speak a much better brand of English than we did back then. But it is sad our kind of Boston pidgin has faded away.

We will just have to close the light on that paht of aah history -- you and I.

ALOHA SNOWBIRDS. HOWZIT?

We are always happy when winter rolls around and the "snowbirds" come back to roost in Kona for awhile. More tennis and golf as well as lots of balls, banquets and parties.

Of course, local businesses delight in the influx of our good friends from the north, and it is great the way our own Rotary Club swells to almost double its normal size with visiting Rotarians from Canada, Alaska, Wisconsin, Minnesota and our northeastern states.

Thank you, "snowbirds," for flying back again to Kona. Aloha nui kako!

THE LOST TRIBE

Our tourists are treated to many interesting stories about the early Hawaiians, both true and untrue. Two tales told by tour drivers on this island (Hawai'i) stretched the imagination a bit.

One is about the long, seemingly endless, rock wall, visible from the Queen Ka'ahumanu Highway, which stretches from the Kawaihae Road across the 'āina toward Kona straight as an arrow as far as the eye can see. It's been said the wall was built by the Menehune (legendary race) in one night. This isn't so, of course. The long lava rock wall was built by the Parker Ranch cowboys under the reign of A.W. Carter, manager of the ranch, way back in the early 1900's.

The next story that gets a little kapakahi (crooked) in the

telling is about Waipi'o Valley, also on the island of Hawai'i. I have heard tour drivers and local musicians refer to the beautiful song Waipi'o as being written about our Hawai'i Island Waipi'o Valley. Not so; the song was written in honor of Francis I'i Brown's family land at Waipi'o on O'ahu. This is land which surrounds Pearl Harbor. This song was the theme song used by Francis during the several times he ran for, (and won), a seat in the Territorial Senate.

As you may know, Francis Brown was into golf in a big way, so whenever he showed up at the clubhouse of a local golf club such as Moanalua, everyone in the place put down his or her can of beer, stood up and sang Waipi'o. As Francis grew older he spent most of his time with Winona Love at his house at Pebble Beach, California. On one of the rare occasions Francis did visit the Moanalua clubhouse in the 1950s, I witnessed a tear in many an eye, as we stood up and sang a full-voiced rendition of the song Waipi'o for him.

The other day I listened to an interesting theory which compared Bible stories with legends told in the ancient days of Hawai'i. My informant, Joe Costelli, said since the stories are so alike, it is the opinion of many that the Hawaiians are the "Lost Tribe of Israel." He stated the Menehune, like Moses, led the Hawaiians to Hawai'i. He noted that, like Adam, Kahiko was the first man. However he used his whole side and not just a rib, to make Wākea, the Hawaiian Eve. Also, the fruit Wākea offered Kahiko was a banana, not an apple.

My storyteller went on to compare Jonah, who lived in a fish, to Kuikuipahu, who lived in the belly of a shark and was let out alive at Hana on Maui. While Pharaoh and Herod were cruel kings mentioned in the Bible, nobody could surpass the cruelty of Hakau who was a half brother of Umi and was chief of Waipi'o. He had the breasts of all females sliced off and had the heads of people with good hair cut off, as well as to have the hands of anyone with good tattoos cut off.

The Hawaiians, like the Israelites, had the rain taken away from them at one time, and as in Hawai'i, also had places of safety or refuge where they could stay and be safe from pursuers. Like the male Jews, the Hawaiians also practiced circumcision, or kahe uli, which was performed using sharp slivers of bamboo.

"Joe," I asked, "where did you pick up all of this information?" He replied he found much of it in Volume V, part III, of the A. Fornander collection of memoirs from the Bernice Pauahi Bishop Museum of Polynesian Ethnology and Natural History. Joe stated the tour groups he leads around in Kona enjoy his "Lost Tribe" theory very much!

BEAN SOUP

One day I ran into Marylou Bean's mother, Mrs. Gouvea, in KTA and her grocery cart was about three-quarters full of packages of dried beans. With a smile on my face, I said, "Mrs. Gouvea, I'm surprised you have to push that cart. It ought to be floating on air!"

Now Mrs. Gouvea is no spring chicken, but she caught on right away and retorted, "No, with beans you don't have a problem with gas. You just soak them in water overnight, and the next day you throw the water away before cooking the beans."

This may be good news for some of you.

KA'AI – A DREAM

Perhaps you will recall articles in the newspapers a while ago about the mysterious disappearance of the remains of two ka'ai (woven sennit mortuary caskets containing bones of high chiefs) from the Bishop Museum in Honolulu. The story quietly died a few weeks later with a vague sort of understanding that the ka'ai were back where they belonged and were well cared for.

For a few months in 1960, Honoka'a Sugar Company rented a helicopter in order to make repairs to the Waipi'o water system which provided water for flumes that carried harvested sugar cane to the mill. It had become too expensive to do repair work with walk-in labor and supplies.

The nice thing about having the helicopter was, in addition to its primary job, the manager of the plantation could quickly survey the condition of growing cane and what not. It was also a dandy way to go on picnics into unexplored beaches and valleys with the family.

One morning, while on an aerial tour of Waipi'o's four mauka (toward the mountains) valleys and the valleys beyond, the sun's rays were just right, and they beamed into a large cave halfway up on the precipitous wall of a valley. For one short moment the manager and the pilot of the helicopter were able to see six shrouded forms lying side by side inside the cave.

Since this was obviously an important burial site, the Honoka'a manager contacted Dr. Kenneth Emory, head archaeologist of the Bishop Museum on O'ahu. An expedition was organized, and within a few weeks, the pilot of the helicopter flew Dr. Emory, a young Hawaiian, and the Honoka'a manager up to the site.

Emory and the Hawaiian, John Kukuihalia, were lowered down to the mouth of the cave using a ladder swinging from beneath the helicopter. The two men stayed down examining the contents of the cave and its shrouded bodies for about four hours. After being brought out, they thanked the plantation manager and pilot, and gave out a vague story about what was going to happen next.

That was the last I heard about this ancient "find." Flying around this same area a few years later, the morning sunlight was perfect and I was able to see into several caves on the sides of the valleys inside Waipi'o. One cave, in particular, had four shrouded figures lined up next to each other.

More recently, according to the daily press, two ka'ai were surreptitiously removed from the Bishop Museum. They were heisted at night, even though there was a guard on duty at the museum, who was presumably awake at the time the ka'ai took a hike.

I had a dream about this. It was as follows: One Alapaki Poloukane Smith had been brought up in Ka-Mo'ili'ili on O'ahu by his Auntie. When he was very young, she told Alapaki that his family, all make (dead) now, were from Niuli'i in Kohala on the Big Island, and were responsible for keeping secret the burial places of high kahuna (priests) and ali'i (chiefs) in North Kohala.

She told him his family line was to eliminate anyone known to have found or disturbed the bones of kings and high priests in the district. She went on to say her nephews' progenitors were very good at killing people with heavy rocks and wooden spears.

Years later, after Alapaki was an adult and had a good job with the telephone company, many people were interested in going back to the old days in Hawai'i. The language, arts, crafts, and lore were revived with a vengeance. The return of lands of the monarchy from the state and federal governments was demanded with much vigor by a number of "sovereignty" groups.

Alapaki was an ardent member of one of these groups, as was John Kukuihalia of the Bishop Museum's staff. They became fast and close friends.

One day after a particularly vigorous demonstration by his group against the theft of land by the government, John told Alapaki he felt very guilty about having helped remove two ka'ai from their resting place in a cave for the Bishop Museum. He said he wished there was some way for him to return them.

Alapaki Smith thought back to the stories he had heard in his youth about his family's sacred trust in protecting the burial sites of the ali'i from robbery. However, he reasoned that killing John with a big rock would not serve a good purpose in this day and age. Besides, a number of other people he did not know were also involved in the original sinful act.

Alapaki, working for the telephone company, knew the company helicopters were often used to string wires and place telephonic equipment in forests and other hard-to-reach places. He wondered if this might be a way of taking the ka'ai back to their sanctuary, if they could be removed from the museum.

He suggested this to his friend Keoni (John), who thought it was a wonderful idea. But how could they find a helicopter pilot who could be trusted to keep silent, should they be able to "free" the ka'ai and take them back. Maybe they should kill the pilot afterwards!

Hamilton "Hambone" Fisher was a security guard at the Bishop Museum. He had been a military policeman with the U.S. Army for most of his adult life and, upon retirement from the Army, going to work as a security officer for the Aloha Security Company was right up his alley.

Hambone worked the night shift inside the museum and the creaking and sighing of the old building didn't bother him, even when he was asleep, which was most of the time. He was not aware John Kukuihalia knew of his habit of napping, and it would be no problem at all to borrow a key for the back door and sneak back in at night, if he and Alapaki only had a helicopter to complete the mission.

Well, it so happened one day, when John was having lunch at the "Family Cafe" on North King Street (serving Hawaiian and Chinese cuisine), he listened to a weather broadcast coming in on the radio from a helicopter pilot on the Big Island.

The pilot sounded like a local boy and so John got to thinking maybe this hot kakala (local expression) was the answer to his problem.

Suddenly I heard my neighbor's dogs barking furiously. They were after a wild pua'a (pig) in my macadamia nut grove. Auwe (alas), what a time to wake up! I was not pau (finished) with my dream.

Mahalo – And Thank Your Very Much

Coming back to Kona from O'ahu several years ago on a Mahalo Airlines' ATR with its wing-on-top-of-the-fuselage kind of airplane, I couldn't help but remember the many trips I made on Aloha Airlines' wing-on-top, F-27 aircraft. Both of these jet-prop planes, with ceiling limits of about 12,000 feet, used to shimmy and shake more than their higher-flying jet buddies. I used to worry the fuselage would become separated from the wings and we would plop down in the ocean. Come to think of it, you wouldn't come out of it any better if the wings on a low-winged plane came off.

Anyway, the flight from Honolulu to Kona was great. It is always nice to see our beautiful islands close up when you are moving along more slowly, and at lower altitudes, than the speedier jets. Besides getting a super view of our fair Hawai'i, the flight took only 15 minutes more, and was much nicer to my pocketbook.

I wish we had another airline like this in Hawai'i today.

An Evening at Hulihe'e Palace

In December one year, we attended a Christmas party at Hulihe'e Palace given by the Kona Hospice. The program was good and the pūpū provided by local restaurants and others were excellent.

At six o'clock, as Hannah Springer, president of our hospice, was welcoming everyone to the party, I chanced to look over the sea wall at all the boats lying tranquilly at anchor in Kailua Bay. A beautiful Kona sunset formed a lovely backdrop for this scene.

At that very moment, the cruise ship S.S. Independence began to move out of the harbor and the twinkling lights of the vessel added a lot to the beauty of the scene.

It was more than a coincidence that I thought about both the Palace and the name of the passenger ship. The words "palace" and "independence" mean different things to different people.

The Mona H

The Mona H was a charter fishing boat at Kailua-Kona until some years ago. She was captained by George Parker, who ran a close second to Captain Henry Chee for the most fish caught in these waters.

George received a lot of fame for bringing in a 1,000-pound plus, black marlin, single-handedly on a trip between Honolulu and Kona after a dry-docking at Hawaiian Tuna packers. Just pause for a minute, you fishermen out there. Can you visualize yourself landing a monster that big alone? Hemingway did his with his Old Man and the Sea.

The Mona H was built at Tuna Packers boatyard and was one of the finest boats with a sampan hull ever built there. Christian Holmes, heir to the Fleishman's Yeast fortune, had it built and named it for his wife, Mona Hind Lucas Holmes.

That was in the mid '30s, just after Chris Holmes had purchased Coconut Island in Kāne'ohe Bay on O'ahu from the B.P. Bishop Estate. What? From the Bishop Estate?

Yes, the Bishop Estate in all of its fame and glory sold out some of its beautiful waterfront property to the yeast heir.

The Mona H carried people and supplies across Kāne'ohe Bay to Coconut Island from a pier at the end of Lilipuna Road. Chris Holmes had transformed Coconut Island into the nearest thing we had in Hawai'i to Disneyland.

There was a small zoo and a sailing ship, the "Seth Parker," which was anchored in cement and rigged with a comfortable bar and movie theater which showed the latest Hollywood movies. The films were brought in weekly on Pan American Airways flying boat, the Mars.

A huge natural salt-water pool had been dug out of the coral on the Kualoa-side of the island facing Chinaman's Hat. Cabanas were provided along one side of the pool for guests to change into their swimming costumes. On the way up to the house, there was a very fancy shooting range designed to look like you were shooting ducks, deer, or bears in Germany's Black Forest.

A two-lane bowling alley was located up near the house and inside was an oversized hikie'e, a Hawaiian couch normally seven feet by seven feet, but this one was over 14 feet x 14 feet, piled high with pillows resting against the wall. There, about eight tired bowlers could relax and be served beverages. In an early labor-saving device, the pin setter doubled as bartender.

The main house at the top of a knoll at the center of the island was octagonal in shape. An inside courtyard was open to the sky and the walls facing the courtyard each held a large saltwater aquarium full of beautiful tropical fish.

People left the island the same way they came; down along a wooden pier extending from shallow to deep water. At the end of this walkway, where one boarded the Mona H, was a small fish "tack" room with its outer walls covered with the toothy grins of 100 or so shark mouths.

Some time after Chris Holmes died, of a self inflicted gunshot wound, the Mona H was sold to George Parker and she became one of Kona's most famous charter fishing boats. Coconut Island was sold to Edwin Pauley of Los Angeles.

NAFTA AT WORK – THE MAUI ROSE POTATO STORY

Some time ago, I listened while an expert reported that the rose potato, which is quite popular in grocery stores these days, was developed on the Island of Moloka'i in the 1960's.

My memory goes back a little further than the '60's and I remember the "Hawaiian" rose potato being sold in the markets before World War II. At the close of the war, Harold Podmore of Honolulu shipped Maui rose potatoes grown at Makawao, Olinda, or someplace like that on Maui, to the U.S. Mainland.

Shipment after shipment, week after week, of these fine Maui rose-colored potatoes left Hawai'i on Matson freighters for sale in California. They were obviously well received, because within a couple of years, California-grown "Maui" rose potatoes began to show up in our Hawaiian markets, week after week.

THE KAKU OF KĪHOLO

According to Dick Frazier, before the 1961 tsunami tore down the banks of the lagoon at Kīholo, a very big kaku (barracuda) lived there. "He was about six feet long," Dick stated.

"Six feet long?" I exclaimed, not exactly believing this fish story. "Yeah, six feet long and mostly mouth with big sharp teeth," he replied.

Dick said the kaku didn't want anyone stealing his private stock of fish. "All you had to do was to stick your foot in the water and that big fish would make a beeline right for you," Dick said.

In those days, the Kīholo Lagoon was full of mullet and huge Samoan crabs with pinchers as big as your hand. Nowadays, with the Ka'ahumanu Highway and other roads nearby, Kīholo is fairly easy to reach for humans. Those fantastic Samoan crabs haven't been seen in years and the bay is now a sanctuary for green turtles. You can see turtle heads bobbing up out of the water all over the place.

You may still find some big fish action at Kīholo if you go swimming at dawn or dusk when the sharks sweep the bay. Sharks like green turtles very much, and they just might like you.

THE AMERICA'S CUP RACE
(FROM JOHNNY NASH'S HOUSE ON BROWN'S BAY)

I call it "America's Cup" but I think it is really "New Zealand's Cup" now. Whether the United States lost it through better crewing by the New Zealand sailors, or through the use of a more efficient computer design in the construction of the New Zealand boat, are questions that are still unanswered. Personally, I think New Zealand had a better crew.

Anyway, Johnny Nash, my old Mānoa Gang pal who had retired to New Zealand, had invited us to come and view the cup race from his house overlooking the ocean where the boats from different nations will challenge each other. Sounded exciting.

On the other hand, Janice Stanger wanted us to go to the summer Olympic games in Australia because her daughter, Maureen, would be on the U.S. Women's water polo team. This and other world class sports challenges would have been great to see, though I didn't know for sure if the Yacht race took place at the same time, or even the same year, "down under." To go to both events would have taken too big a bite out of our purse.

So instead of "another shrimp on the barbee," we went to Turkey.

Hawai'i's Bid for Summer Olympics-

Let's go for it, Hawai'i! But first let's come up with a new state flag. The stars and bars inclusion in the state of Georgia flag caused such a furor that, if the Confederate part of it had not been snipped off, they would not have been allowed to wave it over the 1996 Olympic games in Atlanta.

It would be terrible if athletes and citizens of the U.S.A. boycotted the Olympic Games in fair Hawai'i because our state flag sports the British ensign in the upper left-hand corner.

At the risk of having Hawai'i's flag look like that of a freed Soviet enclave, perhaps we could just drop the British flag out of it and leave the eight stripes.

Maybe the best solution would be to design a completely new flag.

ULU AND PAPAYA

In Thailand, I got used to having young breadfruit (ulu) sliced up and cooked with other vegetables. Here in Hawai'i, if you catch an ulu when it's ripe and about to fall from the tree, you bake it, break it open when it's done, then add butter and lime juice. When I was young, I used to add brown sugar to it, but then I put brown sugar on just about everything, even poi.

Green papaya, skinned and de-seeded, then sliced into thin strips with a vegetable peeler, makes great pūpū when pickled. Be sure to add one of those small red Hawaiian peppers.

A not-quite-ripe papaya, cut in half, cleaned of seeds, is tasty baked. Add brown sugar and lime juice to the cavity before shoving it into the oven resting in a pan with some water on the bottom to prevent drying out.

In the '20's, meat was usually pretty tough, and I remember my mother wrapping it in papaya leaves and leaving it in the refrigerator for 24 hours. I suppose this tenderizing worked, but my teeth back then were young and firm like the rest of me.

JERUSALEM

I imagine many of you remember when Bill Crockett was a member of the Kona Rotary Club. I know Allan Konno and David Rees-Thomas remember Bill well. He was club treasurer and also led us in songs before lunch, "Welcome to Rotareee. . . . ."

Bill had a pet donkey named 'Jerusalem' who won the Kona Jackass races every year. Jerusalem was able to do this because of Bill's long legs, which could reach the pavement while he was in the saddle. This lightened the weight on the beast. Then, if Jerusalem decided he did not want to race, Bill had a pocket full of guess what? No, not carrots, but miniature Milky Ways and Snickers candy bars. Jerusalem would do anything for the candy bars. He did not like Reeses' Cups, though, as the peanut butter stuck to the roof of his mouth.

Jerusalem was loaned to us to help clear out the weeds on our farm when we first moved in. He ate lots of weeds and candy bars. You had to keep your eye on him, though, because he loved to sneak up behind a person and nip him or her on the fanny.

A couple of times while we had Jerusalem, he broke loose and trotted down Walua Road. The first time he got loose, we found him about a block away, and led him home by persuading him with the usual candy bars. The next time he got out he went a little further.... all the way to Emilia Street.

By the time we found him, he was surrounded by lots of people and was enjoying the company very much. As we started to lead him away, an elderly gentleman in the crowd stated he had been a muleskinner in Arkansas, and that our jackasses' hooves were in such poor condition, we must not walk him anywhere.

Looking around at the crowd, I had visions of the police arriving along with the SPCA, so I looked in the yellow pages and found someone to haul Jerusalem home. A week later I returned Jerusalem to Bill Crockett. The next animal I used to clear the weeds ate only diesel oil and would not run away as long as you put on the brakes.

IT'S A FACT

Eventually just about every business or industry fails. We have had loads of them poop out in Hawai'i. To name a few: Tree Fern Mattresses, Cotton, Tobacco, Sisal, Copra, Hardwood Flooring, Fir Christmas Trees, and 'Ōkolehao (Hawaiian Whiskey)

And now, almost all the way out, the sugar and pineapple industries. Our present electric utility and local government are failed businesses, but they will keep on draining resources from our pockets until we become sufficiently tired of it.

Another failed business in Kona is the Kailua Village Plan. Hundreds of thousands of taxpayer dollars have been wasted on study after study. To my knowledge, this waste started in the early '60's and has been going on ever since. The only beneficiary to all of these wasted dollars is the consultant.

Willing, but weak, leadership from our local community, coupled with a passive governmental attitude, is likely to perpetuate this costly study ad infinitum and ad nauseam.

14 ON THE RIGHT – 14 ON THE LEFT

"So, I'll go along and maybe I can help cut up the vegetables for the stew," said Don Simpson as he got up to go with the four or five girls who were going to cook the stew. It was being put together up at the Aloha Café and was to be sold the next day at 75¢ a plate to raise money for the canoe club.

There were about 15 young ladies on our lānai, all making lei for the big Keauhou canoe races the next day. Men, women, junior, senior and novice divisions would all be vying for trophies in the Keauhou to Kailua sprints. The girls were having a wonderful time with much giggling and horsing around as they made haku (woven) lei, and regular ones for all the contestants.

At about 9:30, the "cooks" came back from up mauka with the stew all prepared. Don Simpsons' hand was wrapped in a dish-towel as he had sliced his finger quite badly while cutting carrots. A little paramedical treatment fixed him up quite well though.

The next morning, the girls were quite upset when they found the stew they had made and had left on the stove all night at the Aloha Café had soured. I suggested they sell it as a gourmet-style, sour cream stew, but they didn't think my idea was a very good one. However, in spite of the sour stew, the canoe races went off well and members of the canoe club were happy when it was all over.

Every weekend that summer, we went someplace for the canoe races. When the racing season was over, a big wedding was held for one of the girls. She was marrying a tour driver from Robert's Tours. The wedding was held out in the open, at a little scenic out-look in Keauhou on Ali'i Drive. There were about 100 friends of the couple in attendance with the tour driver's big bus there, engine on and purring away.

Guests who played guitars and 'ukuleles provided home-grown music. Later, during the wedding ceremony, the minister's words were drowned out from time to time when the loud air condi-tioning motor on the bus would kick in. After the ceremony, when asked about the noise, the bridegroom said he wanted to keep the bus cool inside for when he drove away on his honeymoon with his sweetie.

Now that it's the off season for canoe racing, a lot of people are paddling the canoes for exercise. There are many "snowbirds" as well as locals getting in an early morning hour of exercise.

The other day, a pleasant but very much overweight young lady didn't think she could fit into her seat in the canoe. She was finally wedged into place and paddled well, but upon reaching shore at the end of the homeward leg of the paddling exercise, she said she couldn't get out of her canoe seat. It took about four people to pull her loose. I said she was lucky the canoe didn't huli (turn over) when it was out in the deep water off of the Kona Surf Hotel.

"Good to the Last Drop"

A number of years ago, "Good to the last drop!" was used extensively to advertise a brand of coffee. I think it was Maxwell House. Of course, some clown asked, "What's wrong with the last drop?"

This brings to mind a story which happened a few years ago when Mark Rife was president of the Kona Rotary Club. Mark came into possession of a 1957 convertible Chevrolet – a handsome and sporty devil (the car), but with possible unknown problems under the bonnet.

Mark, being the clever guy he is, worked out a deal with Miles, an excellent motor mechanic of this town. They agreed that if Miles kept the car purring along properly until the Rifes moved back to California to be close to their kin, Miles could have the car free.

The Chevy convertible hummed along perfectly for several years. Then, on the day Mark and his wife, Leona, were on the way to the airport to leave Hawai'i, about five miles Kailua side of Keahole Airport the car just quit.

Good to the last drop!

Recipes

The following are some of my favorite recipes. Try them.

Nifty Crab Dish

Two cans crab, mayonnaise, carrots and green pepper cooked and chopped fine. Garlic, salt, pepper. Top with breadcrumbs. Bake 1/2 hr. in a 325°F oven. Best when baked in shells or other dishes with individual servings in each one. Serve as an appetizer for about 6 persons.

Company's Coming - Fast Chicken

1 cut-up chicken (or just thighs or breasts)
1 can of whole cranberries

1 bottle of French dressing
1 package of onion soup mix
1 small can of sliced water chestnuts
Place the chicken in a pan; mix the other ingredients and pour them over the chicken. Bake at 375°F for 1 hour. Serve over rice.

Ulu (Breadfruit) Salad

Although I know most of you have had baked ulu with lemon juice, butter and brown sugar, as well as green, half-ripe ulu boiled with garlic and red pepper, you might try it some time as a substitute for potatoes in potato salad.

First, pick a large green, but almost ripe ulu. Cut off the skin, quarter it and then scoop out and throw away the fibrous core. Boil the remaining ulu gently, for about a half-hour, just like you cook potatoes.

When you can poke a fork into the ulu without too much pilikia (trouble), take it out of the boiling water and cool it on the sink. When it is not too hot to handle, cut it into squares, soak it overnight in oil and vinegar, and the next day mix in mayonnaise, chopped onion, egg and parsley and salt and pepper to taste.

Breadfruit fixed this way will make a softer ride in your 'ōpū (tummy) than potato salad will – I guarantee.

Parmesan Chicken Breasts

6 boneless, skinless chicken breast halves (about 2 pounds)
2 T melted butter
1/2 cup grated Parmesan cheese
1/4 cup dry bread crumbs
1 tsp. each dried oregano leaves and parsley flakes
1/4 tsp. each paprika, salt, and black pepper, and lots of garlic powder.

Heat the oven to 400°F. Spray a 15 x 10 x 1-inch baking pan with no-stick cooking spray. Dip the chicken in the butter; coat with combined remaining ingredients and place in prepared pan. Bake 20 to 25 minutes or until tender. Serves six.

Hawaiian Mexican Good Stuff (Ono!)

6 to 8 pork chops, or about 3 lbs. boned and skinned chicken thighs
1 cup tomato sauce

1 cup tomato paste
2 T chicken bouillon
2 T cumin seed or powder
2 T chili powder
1 T crushed red pepper
1 T salt
1 T large grind black pepper
6 T vegetable oil
1 tsp. sugar
2 cups sliced onions (rings)
1 cup water (add more if sauce gets too thick)
1/2 each red and yellow bell pepper strips (last)

Sauté meat in oil. Mix tomato sauce and paste, all spices, bouillon, and water. Sauté onions until half cooked, add to sautéed meat and then pour tomato and spice mixture over meat and onions. Simmer until almost done on stove or in oven. Add bell pepper strips and serve over brown rice along with a kanaka highball or Primo Beer.

HAWAIIAN "TEXMEX" (SERVES 10 OR SO)

5 lbs. London Broil meat
3 quarts chunky hot salsa
1 tsp sugar

Cut meat into large chunks and place in a pot along with salsa and sugar. Simmer covered for four or five hours until you can shred the meat apart easily. Add Tabasco if not hot enough. Serve with tortillas with a glob of yogurt or sour cream on top or, the way I like it best, in pocket bread.

SACHER TORTE

5 eggs, separated
1/2 cup C&H sugar
4 squares Baker's semisweet chocolate, grated
2 T fine bread crumbs
1 to 3 1/2-oz. package almonds, filberts, or other nuts, ground
1/4 lb. butter, melted and cooled
Red currant or raspberry jam
Chocolate frosting - recipe follows
Whipped cream, rum and powdered sugar (mixed together)

Beat egg whites until stiff, add 1/3 of the sugar and continue beating until rounded peaks are formed. With the same beater, beat egg yolks with remaining sugar until fluffy and lemon colored. Fold grated chocolate, breadcrumbs, egg whites and nuts into the egg yolk mixture until mixed well. Then gently fold in butter.

Bake in two 8 x 8-inch non-stick cake pans in a preheated oven at 350°F for 15 minutes. Lower heat to 300°F and continue baking for 30 minutes or until done. Cake is done when a light touch leaves no impression, or test with a needle or toothpick. Put cake on a rack to cool. Run spatula gently around the sides and turn cake onto a platter. When completely cool, spread jam over the top and sides and pour chocolate icing over. Serve with whipped cream.

This is believed to be the original and best recipe from the famous Sacher Hotel in Vienna. This hotel was once the meeting place of the "high class" and "elegant" with gourmet tastes.

Chocolate Icing Frosting:

1 large bar (8-10 oz.) semisweet chocolate
2 to 3 T light fresh olive oil.

Melt chocolate in double boiler. Slowly add oil. Cook till melted then pour over Sacher Torte

Here I am with my mother, Geraldine Mary Francis Neumann Collins, during one of many visits to San Francisco.

*With my parents George Miles Collins and Geraldine
Collins in our new home in Mānoa on Kahawai Street.*

On the Punahou football team.

I'm the tall guy. With me are my friends Johnny Nash and Roger Monsarrat. We're camping in the pine forest, Kailua, O'ahu.

Surfing at Kailua Beach on O'ahu.

On Lanikai Beach, 1952, with The Sultan of Lanikai.

I managed to work in the pineapple canneries, but could also put on a tux when I had to.

Here's one of those work-related head shots, taken about the time some of us were painting green stripes down Kalākaua Avenue.

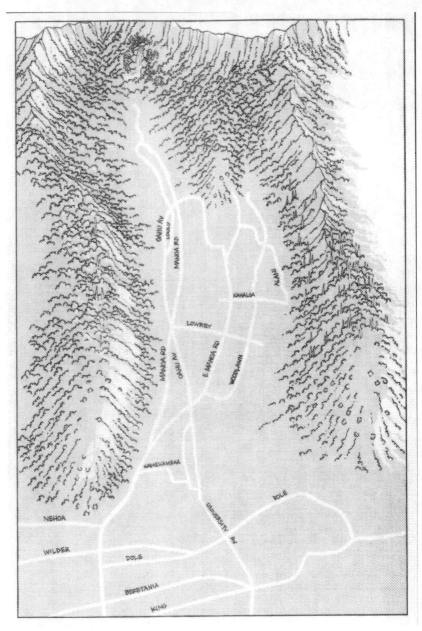

Map of Mānoa Valley, circa 1900.

The waterfalls of Mānoa Valley, circa 1930. (Bishop Museum Archives)

Mānoa Valley in 1924. (Photo by 11 Photo Section, Air Service, USA, Bishop Museum Achives)

The Mānoa Valley Trolley. I used to ride on the rear cow catcher or on the outside steps. This was good for a quick exit before the conductor reached me for my nickel fare. (Hawaii State Archives)

Mānoa Market circa 1953. I used to buy candy here all the time. (Photo by Camera Hawaii, Bishop Museum Archives)

Ship passengers with lei as they arrive at Honolulu Harbor circa 1935. (Photo by N.R. Farbman, Bishop Museum Archives)

Moana Hotel on Waikiki Beach, 1924. (Bishop Museum Archives)

At left is the Outrigger Canoe Club in 1922 with canoes stored under the pavillion. At center is the Moana Hotel. (Bishop Museum Archives)

I took surfing and canoe lessons from David Kahanamoku, third from right, the oldest of the Kahanamoku brothers. I remember running up and down the pier in front of the Moana Hotel seen here. Duke is on the far right. (Photo by Tai Sing Loo, 1931, Bishop Museum Archives)

The gate to the Chinese graveyard near the bridge where I used to hide during funeral processions. (Hawaii State Archives)

Kailua-Kona circa 1895. (Hawaii State Archives)

Aerial view of Kailua-Kona circa 1960. (Hawaii State Archives)

Kona Nightingales. Coffee growers used them years ago during harvest season. Now they're mostly just wild.

"Pinetrees" - a favorite surfing spot near Kailua-Kona.

Loading cattle from Parker Ranch onto sailing freighters. (Hawaii State Archives)

Parker Ranch circa 1920. (Hawaii State Archives)

Parker Ranch circa 1920. (Hawaii State Archives)